THE
VEGGIE
COOKBOOK

THE
VEGGIE
COOKBOOK

120 GLORIOUS
EVERYDAY RECIPES

CAMILLA STEPHENS

MITCHELL BEAZLEY

An Hachette UK Company
www.hachette.co.uk

First published in Great Britain in 2019 by Mitchell Beazley,
an imprint of Octopus Publishing Group Ltd, Carmelite House,
50 Victoria Embankment, London EC4Y 0DZ
www.octopusbooks.co.uk
www.octopusbooksusa.com

Distributed in the US by Hachette Book Group, 1290 Avenue of the Americas,
4th and 5th Floors, New York, NY 10104

Distributed in Canada by Canadian Manda Group, 664 Annette St, Toronto,
Ontario, Canada M6S 2C8

ISBN 978-1-78472-492-4

A CIP catalogue record for this book is available from the British Library.

Printed and bound in China.

10 9 8 7 6 5 4 3 2 1

Group Publishing Director: Denise Bates
Art Director: Yasia Williams-Leedham
Senior Editor: Leanne Bryan
Production Controller: Gemma Nic
Initial Design Concept: Nicola Ansell & Ariel Cortese
Cover Design: Nicola Ansell & Ariel Cortese
Photography: Dan Jones
Illustrator: Hannah Turpin
Make-up Artist: Victoria Barnes
Food styling: Georgina Fuggle & Anna Shepherd
Prop styling: Tonia Shuttleworth

CONTENTS

INTRODUCTION

So, who's this book for? Maybe you're a committed vegetarian who has become bored with their recipe repertoire and is looking to learn a few new tricks and bring some bold new flavours into their cooking. Or perhaps you've begun dallying with the idea of meat-free Mondays and are searching for some seriously good recipes to inspire you.

Or maybe you're more like me: somewhere in between. A bit – dare I say it? – flexitarian. You do eat meat and fish but you're committed to the idea of eating more veg, and you would like the children to eat more too.

Whichever camp you fall in, my ambition is that this book will zhoosh things up in your kitchen and help you to experiment with veggies in a new way.

As with any type of cooking, different occasions call for different approaches, and in this book there is a chapter for every eventuality. In Everyday Veg (see page 9), you'll find tried and tested family favourites, each of them simple to make and a bona fide hit with the children. Like my foolproof Meat-free Monday Lasagne (see page 18), with its slightly charred, crisp edges and soft, deeply savoury inside layers, or my crowd-pleasing Corner-shop Samosas (see page 28), for which everything can be sourced very locally indeed.

In Fast Veg (see page 43) I'll show how trusted shortcuts such as deli charred artichokes and posh pre-cooked grains can help you fling a veggie meal together in a matter of minutes. If you think that after a manic Monday you'll have no time to cook, my 20-minute Pantry-to-plate Pappardelle (see page 58) may well prove you wrong.

For occasions when you have a little more time on your hands and you're keen to impress, Veg Feasts (see page 69) is packed with real showstoppers, the Whole Roasted Coconut Cauliflower with Crispy Potatoes & Greens on page 79 being a particular winner. And should the honour of hosting Christmas dinner fall to you this year, the Cranberry and Porcini Nut Roast on page 89, with its intensely flavoured porcini mushrooms, sweet butternut squash and tangy cranberries, is sure to provide a whole new perspective on the vegetarian staple, which often gets bad press.

Because more and more of us are eating on the hop, I've dedicated the Veg on the Go chapter to hearty, wholesome snacks (see page 137). These are the kind of recipes you can make on a rainy afternoon, then pop into lunchboxes or take on picnics, such as my zingy Corn & Feta Muffins (see page 149) or my Scotch Veg Eggs complete with a Tomato Chutney for dipping (see page 141) – a joyous (and guilt-free) riff on the service-station staple.

Towards the end of the book, I turn my attention to Sweet Treats (see page 173). Now, I do realize this is a tad cheeky – after all, how many desserts feature meat or fish? Well, in my defence, all the recipes in this chapter let fruit take centre stage – or, in some cases veg, such as the Courgette & Lemon Poppy Seed Bars on page 194, which my children adore. So hopefully you can find it in your heart to forgive me, and if I can't persuade you, perhaps the Orange and Rosemary Upside-down Cake on page 174 will.

Last of all, I cover useful stuff like sauces and dressings, and include a super-handy recipe for a veggie Onion Gravy (see page 216). And, of course, no Higgidy cookbook would be complete without a few words on how to make peerless Savoury Shortcrust Pastry (see page 206).

Although a typical day at Higgidy often involves taste-testing new recipes, the majority of my cooking and experimenting actually takes place in my kitchen at home. And, I can honestly say that during the journey of writing this book, I've found myself (and my family) enjoying cooking and eating more veg than ever before. I hope that I can inspire you to do the same.

EVERYDAY VEG

Weekday suppers call for friendly, approachable recipes; meals that are easy on the cook and a hit with the kids. A serious Bolognese, with heaps of hidden veg, perhaps. Or a proper veggie burger.

EAT YOUR GREENS FILO PIE

We have a saying at Higgidy: 'Everything's better with feta.' The cheese's rich zinginess seems to enhance the flavour of whatever you pair with it, greens being a particular firm friend. This zesty version of the classic Greek spanakopita is wonderful served warm, and when cooled and cut into wedges it makes a great lunchbox zhoosher-upper. It's great served with thinly sliced cucumber tossed with a little dill and some freshly squeezed lemon juice.

SERVES 6

EQUIPMENT: 1 rectangular loose-bottomed tart tin, 20 × 30cm

500g spring greens, Swiss chard or baby kale, or a mixture of all three

2 tablespoons olive oil

1 onion, finely chopped

1 small bunch of spring onions, white and green parts finely sliced

Grated zest of 1 unwaxed lemon

1 small bunch of dill, leaves picked and finely chopped

1 small bunch of flat leaf parsley, leaves picked and finely chopped

3 eggs, beaten

200g feta cheese, crumbled

50g unsalted butter

7 sheets of filo pastry, defrosted and kept covered in a clean tea towel if frozen

Salt and freshly ground black pepper

1. Preheat the oven to 200°C/180°C fan/Gas Mark 6. If the greens have not been pre-washed, give them a really good wash, then drain. Tear the leaves from any tough white stalks (particularly with spring greens). Place the greens in a large saucepan with a few tablespoons of water and a pinch of salt, cover the pan with a lid and cook over a low heat for a few minutes until they have shrunk down and wilted. Pour into a colander and leave to cool for a few minutes. Use your hands to squeeze as much water from the greens as you can, then roughly chop them and tip into a large mixing bowl.

2. Heat the olive oil in a small frying pan, add the onion with a pinch of salt and sauté over a medium heat for 5–7 minutes until softened but not browned. Add the spring onion and cook for a further 4 minutes. Add the onion mixture to the chopped greens along with the lemon zest and herbs. Season generously with salt and pepper. Stir well so that the seasoning and the herbs are evenly mixed through the greens.

3. Mix the eggs and feta together in a separate mixing bowl, then stir the mixture into the greens. Don't be tempted to overmix, as it's lovely to taste some chunks of feta when the pie is warm.

4. Melt the butter in a small saucepan. Brush the tart tin with the melted butter and arrange a sheet of filo pastry in the base, allowing the excess pastry to overhang the edges of the tin. Brush the filo with melted butter. Lay 3 more sheets of filo over the top, brushing each sheet all over with butter as you go. Pack the filling into the pastry case, then fold the edges of the pastry sheets into the middle of the pie and arrange the final 3 sheets of filo over the top. Using a sharp knife, lightly score the top of the pie in a criss-cross pattern.

5. Bake for 30 minutes or until the filo is golden and crisp and the filling is piping hot. Remove the pie from the oven and leave to cool slightly before cutting into squares.

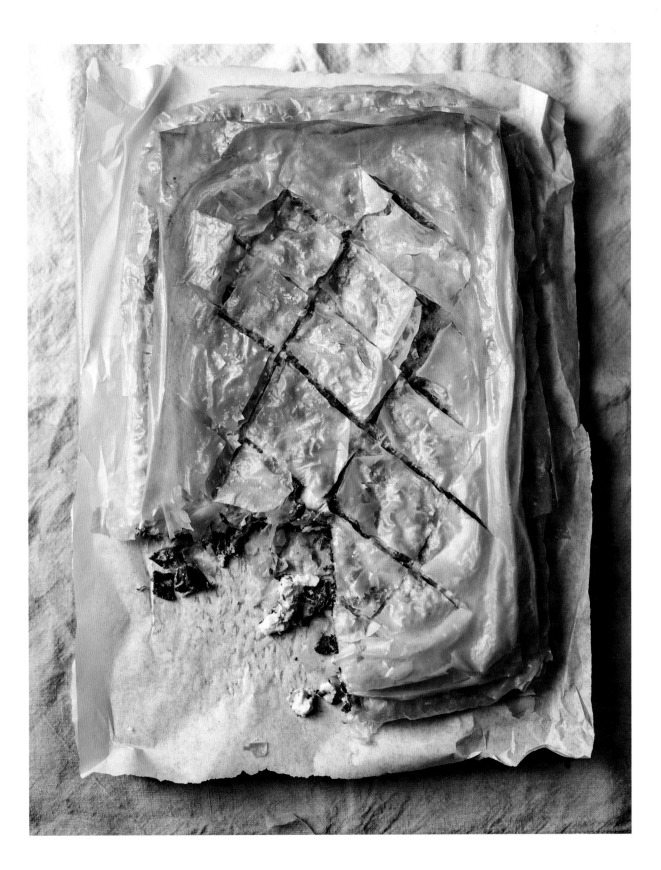

VEG-PACKED BOLOGNESE

Whether you're a diehard veggie or a card-carrying carnivore, you need some sort of Bolognese in your life. Richly flavoured, warming and healthy, it's one of those freezer-friendly dishes whose mere presence in the freezer will put a spring in your step. Take it out the night before and you can have a super-tasty meal on the table in the time it takes to cook the spaghetti.

SERVES 4-6

25g dried porcini mushrooms

300ml warm water

2 tablespoons olive oil

1 onion, finely chopped

2 carrots, peeled and finely diced

2 celery sticks, finely diced

2 garlic cloves, finely sliced

3 bay leaves

400g can green or black lentils, drained and rinsed

600ml passata (sieved tomatoes)

1 teaspoon mild dried chilli flakes

1 teaspoon light muscovado sugar

2 tablespoons balsamic vinegar

1 small bunch of oregano, leaves picked

To serve

Cooked spaghetti

Grated Parmesan cheese

1. Place the dried porcini mushrooms in a bowl and cover with the measured warm water. Leave to soak for 20 minutes.

2. Meanwhile, heat the olive oil in a large, heavy-based saucepan, add the onion, carrots and celery with a pinch of salt and sauté over a low heat for 15 minutes until soft.

3. Strain the soaked porcini through a fine sieve over a bowl to catch the soaking liquid. Roughly chop the porcini and add them along with the garlic to the vegetables in the pan. Cook over a medium heat, stirring regularly, for 3–4 minutes.

4. Add all the remaining ingredients except the oregano and season with salt and pepper. Pour the reserved porcini soaking liquid into the pan, stir well and bring to the boil, then reduce the heat, cover the pan with a lid and gently simmer for 25 minutes until the sauce has thickened. Stir the oregano leaves through the Bolognese, and taste and adjust the seasoning.

5. Using a potato masher, mash the Bolognese in the pan for a minute until some of the lentils and vegetables have broken down to create a textured sauce.

6. Serve the Bolognese with cooked spaghetti for a veggie take on spag bol, sprinkled with generous handfuls of grated Parmesan cheese.

TIP

LENTILS ARE A GOOD SOURCE OF FIBRE AND PROTEIN, WHICH MAKES THEM BRILLIANT FOR VEGETARIANS AND GROWING CHILDREN.

SWEET POTATO CRUSTED COTTAGE PIE

For me, the best vegetable dishes are those that make clever use of bold flavours and hearty textures. This one, with its umami-rich Worcester sauce and red wine, and its sustaining lentils and cannellini beans, is no less satisfying than the traditional meaty version.

SERVES 6

EQUIPMENT: 1 × 2-litre ovenproof pie dish

2 tablespoons olive oil

1 large red onion, diced

2 celery sticks, diced

2 carrots, peeled and diced

2 garlic cloves, finely chopped

1½ teaspoons paprika

¼ teaspoon ground mace

4 large tomatoes, roughly chopped, or 400g can chopped tomatoes

2 bay leaves

5 sprigs of thyme, leaves picked

100g dried red lentils

400g can cannellini beans

150ml red wine

1 teaspoon vegetable bouillon powder or ½ vegetable stock cube

1 tablespoon vegetarian Worcester sauce

Salt and freshly ground black pepper

For the sweet potato mash

900g sweet potatoes, peeled and cut into 3cm chunks

50g unsalted butter

1 tablespoon wholegrain mustard

100g mature Cheddar cheese, grated

1. Heat the olive oil in a deep saucepan, add the onion, celery and carrot and sprinkle over a pinch of salt. Cover the pan with a lid and sweat the vegetables over a low heat, stirring occasionally, for 15 minutes until soft.

2. Add the garlic to the pan along with the paprika and mace, turn the heat up to medium and toast the spices for a minute. Stir in the tomatoes, bay and thyme. Cover the pan again and cook for a further 7–8 minutes until the tomatoes have collapsed and started to release some of their liquid. Stir in the lentils, the can of beans with their liquid and the wine. Add the bouillon powder or stock cube to the empty bean can and fill with boiling water from the kettle, stirring. Pour the stock into the pan along with the Worcester sauce. Bring the contents of the pan to the boil, then reduce the heat, cover with the lid and simmer gently for 20 minutes until the sauce has started to thicken. Remove the lid and simmer for a further 10 minutes to evaporate some of the liquid. Discard the bay leaves and set aside.

3. While the lentil and bean mixture is simmering, preheat the oven to 200°C/180°C fan/Gas Mark 6. To prepare the mash, bring a large saucepan of water to the boil. Add a pinch of salt and the sweet potato chunks and boil for 15–20 minutes until completely soft. Drain the sweet potatoes and return to the pan. Add the butter, mustard and half the Cheddar, then use a potato masher to mash the sweet potatoes until completely smooth. Set aside.

4. Once the lentil and bean mixture is ready, use the same potato masher as before (don't worry about washing it) to mash about half of it in the saucepan. Taste and adjust the seasoning with salt and pepper.

5. Spoon the lentil and bean mixture into the pie dish. Spread the sweet potato mash over the top and sprinkle over the remaining Cheddar. Bake for 25 minutes until golden and bubbling. Serve hot.

POPPED BEAN & TOMATO TRAYBAKE

After a manic Monday, this is one of my favourite suppers to cook. Once you've got everything chopped, it's simply a case of bunging it in the oven, and the accompanying Tahini Sauce is also a cinch to prepare. What's more, the quantities are extremely forgiving, so if you happen to have less broccoli and more tomatoes, for example, it will still work brilliantly.

SERVES 3–4

2 sweet potatoes, peeled and cut into irregular-shaped 3cm chunks

6 tomatoes, roughly chopped

1 red onion, sliced into thin wedges

2 garlic cloves, finely sliced

3 sprigs of rosemary or thyme

2 tablespoons sherry vinegar

6 tablespoons olive oil

400g can cannellini beans, drained

250g Tenderstem broccoli, cut into 3cm lengths

1 teaspoon fennel seeds

Grated zest and juice of 1 unwaxed lemon

Salt and freshly ground black pepper

To serve

1 quantity of Tahini Sauce (see page 211)

4 flatbreads, warmed (optional)

1. Preheat the oven to 220°C/200°C fan/Gas Mark 7.

2. Tumble the sweet potatoes, tomatoes, onion, garlic and rosemary or thyme together in a deep roasting tin. Drizzle over the vinegar and 4 tablespoons of the olive oil to coat the vegetables. Season well with salt and pepper and cover the tin tightly with foil. Roast on the middle shelf of the oven for 25 minutes.

3. Spread the beans out in a single layer on a baking tray. Drizzle with the remaining 2 tablespoons of olive oil and season with salt and pepper.

4. Remove the roasting tin from the oven, carefully peel away the foil and use a spatula or wooden spoon to gently crush the tomatoes. Stir through the broccoli and fennel seeds, then return the roasting tin to the middle shelf of the oven, placing the beans on the top shelf at the same time, and roast for a further 20 minutes until the vegetables are soft and charring at the edges.

5. Remove the beans and vegetables from the oven, then scoop the beans on top of the veggies and scatter over the lemon zest and juice. Give everything a really good stir before serving with the Tahini Sauce and warmed flatbreads, if liked.

MEAT-FREE MONDAY LASAGNE

It wouldn't surprise me if people outside of Italy ate more lasagne than they do in its home country. Perhaps it's the contrast of slightly charred, crisp edges with soft, deeply savoury layers within that makes it so appealing, which is equally the case in this veggie version. Once you've made the Bolognese sauce, this dish is very straightforward to put together. Serve it with a salad or some wilted greens.

SERVES 6

EQUIPMENT: 1 × 20cm square ovenproof dish or roasting tin

For the cheese sauce

50g unsalted butter, plus a little extra for greasing

50g plain flour

700ml milk

50g Parmesan cheese, grated

Salt and freshly ground black pepper

For the lasagne

1 quantity of Veg-packed Bolognese (see page 13)

150g mascarpone cheese

200g dried lasagne sheets

3 sprigs of oregano, leaves picked

20g Parmesan cheese, grated

1. Preheat the oven to 200°C/180°C fan/Gas Mark 6.

2. To make the cheese sauce, melt the butter in a medium saucepan until it starts to bubble and stir in the flour with a wooden spoon. Cook over a medium heat for about a minute, stirring regularly, until the mixture has turned a shade darker and smells toasty. Gradually add the milk and whisk continuously until the sauce has thickened and coats the back of the spoon. Remove the pan from the heat, add the Parmesan and stir until it has melted. Taste the sauce and season with salt and pepper.

3. Lightly grease the ovenproof dish or roasting tin with butter. Spoon one-third of the Bolognese evenly over the base of the dish or tin, then use the spoon to dot one-third of the mascarpone evenly over it. Top with one-third of the lasagne sheets to completely cover the Bolognese mixture, breaking them into pieces to fill the gaps if necessary. Repeat with the remaining Bolognese, mascarpone and lasagne sheets, finishing with a layer of lasagne sheets on top.

4. Pour the cheese sauce over the top layer of lasagne sheets and arrange the oregano leaves over the sauce. Scatter the Parmesan evenly over the lasagne and bake for 35 minutes until golden and bubbling. Serve hot.

AUBERGINE & PEARL BARLEY MOUSSAKA

This is what I describe as 'box set food', the sort of dish that's ideal for making
on a quiet afternoon to pop in the freezer and then enjoy on a Friday night in front
of your favourite TV series. The pearl barley brings a nice nuttiness to the proceedings
and makes this moussaka even heartier than the traditional meat version.

SERVES 6

EQUIPMENT: 1 rectangular ovenproof
dish, 20 × 30cm

150g pearl barley

2 aubergines, cut lengthways into
1cm-thick slices

50ml olive oil, plus extra for drizzling

2 red onions, finely chopped

1 red pepper, cored, deseeded and
chopped into 1cm dice

3 garlic cloves, finely sliced

2 tablespoons tomato purée

1 cinnamon stick

1 teaspoon fennel seeds

150g carrots, peeled and grated

A few sprigs of thyme or oregano,
leaves picked and roughly chopped

400g can chopped tomatoes

3 tablespoons red wine vinegar

Salt and freshly ground black pepper

For the topping

250g ricotta cheese

200g Greek yogurt

3 eggs, lightly beaten

30g Parmesan or pecorino cheese, grated

⅛ whole nutmeg, grated

Salt and freshly ground black pepper

1. Cook the pearl barley according to the pack instructions, then drain and set aside.

2. Toss the aubergine slices with the olive oil and a generous pinch of salt and pepper in a large mixing bowl. Heat a large frying pan over a medium heat and cook the aubergines, in batches, for 3–4 minutes on each side until golden brown and softened. Set aside.

3. Wipe out the pan with a piece of kitchen paper, add a drizzle of olive oil and then the onions and red pepper with a pinch of salt and sauté, stirring regularly, for about 8 minutes until they have softened.

4. Stir in the garlic, tomato purée, cinnamon stick and fennel seeds and toast the spices for a minute until they release their fragrance before adding the carrots, herbs, tomatoes and vinegar. Half-fill the tomato can with water, add to the pan and stir to combine, then gently simmer the mixture, uncovered, for 20–25 minutes until it has thickened. Taste and adjust the seasoning with salt and pepper before stirring through the cooked pearl barley.

5. Preheat the oven to 200°C/180°C fan/Gas Mark 6. Spread half the barley and vegetable mixture in the ovenproof dish. Arrange half the aubergine slices over the top, then add the remaining barley and vegetable mixture and cover with the remaining aubergine slices.

6. Beat all the ingredients for the topping together in a mixing bowl until well combined, then spread the mixture evenly over the top layer of aubergine. Bake for 35 minutes or until the topping is golden and bubbling at the sides. Serve hot.

BLACK BEAN VEGGIE BURGERS

These burgers pack in some serious flavour. And they're really not difficult to make; after a quick blitz of the ingredients in the food processor, it's a simple case of shaping the mixture into neat patties and crisping them up in a frying pan.

MAKES 6

For the burgers

2 × 400g cans black beans, drained and well rinsed

2 teaspoons yeast extract (such as Marmite)

1 egg, beaten

1 teaspoon wholegrain mustard

1 teaspoon light brown soft sugar

3 tablespoons roughly chopped flat leaf parsley

75g rolled porridge oats

75g Cheddar cheese, finely grated

2–3 tablespoons olive oil

To serve

Thick slices of beef tomato

Your favourite ketchup

Crisp lettuce leaves

1. Add the black beans to a food processor with the yeast extract, beaten egg, mustard and brown sugar and blitz to form a soft mixture. Spoon the mixture into a mixing bowl and stir through the parsley, oats and Cheddar. Leave the mixture to sit in the fridge for 30 minutes to absorb the moisture and allow the flavours to develop.

2. Shape the chilled burger mixture, which should be thick and pliable, into 6 thick patties about the size of a digestive biscuit (about 6cm). Brush the patties on both sides with the olive oil until evenly covered.

3. Heat a non-stick frying pan over a medium–high heat, add the burgers and fry for 8 minutes on each side or until they are crispy on the outside and hot all the way through.

4. Serve the burgers immediately with beef tomato slices, a touch of ketchup and some crisp lettuce leaves.

ROASTED CAULIFLOWER & CHICKPEA CURRY

As the recipe title suggests, this is not a curry of the blow-your-head-off variety. I love a good vindaloo as much as the next person, but I often crave something mellower, more Zen. With its warm, fragrant mix of spices, this dish will fill your kitchen with the most amazing aromas.

SERVES 4–6

3 tablespoons coconut oil, melted

1 large cauliflower, cut into bite-sized florets

3 teaspoons ground cumin

1 teaspoon ground coriander

¼ teaspoon ground cinnamon

2 onions, finely chopped

1 small thumb of fresh root ginger, peeled and finely grated

1 red chilli, deseeded and finely chopped

1 small bunch of coriander, stalks and leaves separated

1 teaspoon black mustard seeds

1 teaspoon fenugreek seeds

1 teaspoon ground turmeric

3 tomatoes, roughly chopped

400ml can coconut milk

400g can chickpeas, drained and rinsed

100g baby spinach, washed

Juice of 1 lime

Salt and freshly ground black pepper

Naan breads or cooked rice, to serve

1. Preheat the oven to 200°C/180°C fan/Gas Mark 6.

2. Pour half the melted coconut oil into a shallow roasting tin, add the cauliflower florets and toss to coat with the oil. Add 2 teaspoons of the cumin, the coriander and cinnamon and some salt and pepper, then toss again to evenly coat the cauliflower. Roast for 25 minutes until the cauliflower is cooked through and charring at the edges. Remove from the oven and set aside.

3. While the cauliflower is roasting, heat the remaining coconut oil in a deep saucepan, add the onions with a pinch of salt and sauté over a medium heat for 7–8 minutes until soft and translucent but not browned. Add the ginger and chilli, then chop the coriander stalks and add these too, reserving the coriander leaves for later. Cook, stirring continuously, for a couple of minutes, then add the mustard and fenugreek seeds and cook for a minute or so. Stir through the remaining cumin and the turmeric and cook for a further minute or until the spices smell fragrant, then add the tomatoes.

4. Continue to cook the curry base for 5 minutes or until the tomatoes have started to break down and you have a rough curry paste.

5. Add the coconut milk and chickpeas and bring the contents of the pan to a gentle simmer. Cook over a low–medium heat for 25 minutes until the sauce has thickened.

6. Stir the roasted cauliflower and spinach through the curry, then remove the pan from the heat (the spinach will continue to cook in the residual heat). Season the curry with the lime juice and salt and pepper to taste. Scatter over the reserved coriander leaves and serve in warmed bowls with naan breads or rice.

HIDDEN VEGETABLE PILAF

Some of my favourite dishes are those that slowly reveal themselves as they cook. This hands-free, oven-baked pilaf, with its heady harissa, fragrant cumin and sweet cinnamon, will fill your home with the evocative aromas of North Africa while you put your feet up for a well-earned rest.

SERVES 4

EQUIPMENT: 1 large ovenproof frying pan or 3-litre shallow ovenproof casserole pan

4 tablespoons olive oil

2 red onions, finely chopped

2 celery sticks, finely chopped

2 parsnips (about 200g), peeled and finely chopped

3 garlic cloves, chopped

1 teaspoon dried thyme leaves

1 tablespoon harissa paste

2 teaspoons ground cumin

½ teaspoon ground cinnamon

½ swede (about 200g), peeled and grated

½ celeriac (about 200g), peeled and grated

200g brown rice

400g can chopped tomatoes

50g dried cranberries

600ml vegetable stock

30g pistachio nuts, roughly chopped

100g feta cheese

A handful of flat leaf parsley leaves, chopped

1 lemon, cut into wedges

Salt and freshly ground black pepper

1. Preheat the oven to 200°C/180°C fan/Gas Mark 6.

2. Heat the olive oil in the frying or casserole pan, add the onions, celery and parsnips and sauté over a medium heat for about 8 minutes until soft.

3. Add the garlic, thyme, harissa and spices to the pan and cook for a couple of minutes. Stir in the grated swede and celeriac with a pinch of salt and some pepper and cook, stirring regularly, for 5–7 minutes until the vegetables have softened.

4. Push the vegetables to the side of the pan with a wooden spoon and scatter the rice in the centre. Gently turn the rice with the spoon, lightly toasting it for a couple of minutes until it starts to smell nutty.

5. Add the tomatoes, cranberries and vegetable stock and stir to combine. Bring the contents of the pan to the boil, then reduce the heat and simmer for 5 minutes to get everything going before transferring the pan to the middle shelf of the oven. Bake for 35 minutes.

6. Remove the pan from the oven, scatter over the pistachios and crumble the feta on top in irregular-sized chunks. Bake the pilaf for a further 15 minutes until the feta is golden and the rice is plumped up and cooked through.

7. Serve in warmed bowls with the parsley scattered over the top and the lemon wedges for squeezing over.

SQUASH MAC & CHEESE PIE

Like many mums, I've developed a knack for hiding veg in food – a skill that has come into its own while writing this book. And with this mac and cheese pie, which features an entire butternut squash on 'covert ops', I may have reached the pinnacle of my stealth skills. Kids love it.

SERVES 6–8

EQUIPMENT: 1 × 23cm round springform cake tin

1 butternut or queen squash (about 1kg), peeled, deseeded and cut into 3cm chunks

6 tablespoons extra virgin olive oil, plus extra for drizzling

1 onion, cut into 8 wedges

3 garlic cloves, unpeeled

5 sprigs of thyme, leaves picked

5 sprigs of rosemary

1 teaspoon pul biber (Turkish dried chilli flakes), or ½ teaspoon dried chilli flakes

½ teaspoon salt

1 heaped teaspoon Dijon mustard

400g dried macaroni

75g unsalted butter, melted

9 sheets (2 packets) of filo pastry, defrosted and kept covered in a clean tea towel if frozen

Salt and freshly ground black pepper

For the white sauce

50g unsalted butter

50g plain flour

750ml milk

⅛ whole nutmeg, grated

150g Cheddar cheese, grated

1. Preheat the oven to 200°C/180°C fan/Gas Mark 6.

2. Toss the squash with 3 tablespoons of the olive oil, the onion, garlic, herbs, chilli flakes and salt in a roasting tin and roast for 40 minutes, turning twice during this time, until the squash is charred at the edges and soft to the point of a knife. Remove from the oven and leave to cool, keeping the oven on. Once cool enough to handle, remove and discard the rosemary. Pop the garlic cloves out of their skins into a food processor along with the roasted squash and onion and the mustard and blitz until the vegetables have broken down. While the processor is running on a high speed, pour in the remaining olive oil and blend until smooth.

3. For the white sauce, melt the butter in a saucepan and stir in the flour. Cook over a medium heat for about a minute, stirring regularly, until the mixture has turned a shade darker and smells toasty. Gradually add the milk and the nutmeg and whisk continuously until the sauce has thickened. Remove the pan from the heat, add the Cheddar and stir until it has melted. Taste and season the sauce with salt and pepper.

4. Bring a large saucepan of water to the boil and add a pinch of salt. Add the macaroni and boil for 6 minutes until al dente. Scoop out a mugful of the pasta cooking water before draining the pasta in a colander, then return the pasta to the pan with the reserved water and stir well. Add the squash mixture and cheese sauce and stir until all the macaroni is evenly coated.

5. Brush the base and sides of the tin with melted butter to grease. Drape a sheet of filo pastry over the tin, pushing it into the sides and down to the base, allowing any excess to overhang the edges. Brush the first sheet of filo with melted butter, then turn the tin 90° and add another sheet. Brush with butter and repeat with another 5 sheets. Pour the macaroni mixture into the centre of the tin. Drape the overhanging filo over the top of the mixture, brushing each sheet with melted butter as you go. Top with the remaining 2 sheets of filo to cover the centre of the pie and brush with melted butter. Bake the pie for 30–35 minutes until the filo is deep golden.

6. Remove the pie from the oven and leave to cool for 15 minutes before releasing it from the tin, by which point it will be much easier to slice.

GARDEN PEA & NEW POTATO QUICHE

I'm not sure if it's the sweet green peas or the tender baby potatoes, but my children adore this quiche. Bright and springlike, with lovely little bursts of flavour from the dollops of herby green pesto, would it be too cheeky to think of it as one of our five-a-day?

SERVES 6

EQUIPMENT: 1 × 23cm round loose-bottomed fluted tart tin

1 quantity of Savoury Shortcrust Pastry (see page 206), or use ready-made shortcrust pastry, defrosted if frozen

A little plain flour, for dusting

Mixed salad leaves, to serve

For the filling

1 garlic bulb, cloves separated (about 15) and peeled

3 tablespoons olive oil

1 tablespoon balsamic vinegar

400g baby new potatoes, large ones halved and smaller ones quartered

150g frozen peas

1 small bunch of flat leaf parsley, leaves picked

4 eggs

125ml double cream

3 tablespoons good-quality shop-bought pesto

Salt and freshly ground black pepper

1. Unless using ready-made pastry, make the Savoury Shortcrust Pastry following the method on page 206, then wrap in cling film and leave to rest in the fridge for 30 minutes.

2. Roll the pastry out on a lightly floured surface into a round about 3mm thick and line your tin with it, making sure the edges of the pastry stand a little proud above the rim of the tin. Trim the edges to even and prick the base all over with a fork, then chill the pastry case in the fridge for 30 minutes. Meanwhile, preheat the oven to 200°C/180°C fan/Gas Mark 6 with a baking sheet inside.

3. Line the pastry case with non-stick baking paper and fill it with dried beans, uncooked rice or ceramic baking beans. Bake the pastry case on the hot baking sheet for 15 minutes. Remove the paper and baking beans or rice and then bake the pastry case for a further 15 minutes to ensure that the base is cooked. Remove from the oven and set aside to cool.

4. Toss the garlic cloves in the olive oil in a small shallow roasting tin. Cover tightly with foil and roast for 15 minutes. Remove the tin from the oven and pour over the vinegar, then roast for a further 5 minutes until the garlic is golden in places and soft throughout. Remove from the oven, keeping the oven on.

5. Bring a large saucepan of well-salted water to the boil, lower in the potatoes and boil for 12–15 minutes until a sharp knife passes through them easily. Just before the potatoes are done, add the peas to the pan and boil for 1 minute or until they rise to the surface. Drain the potatoes and peas in a colander and leave them to sit and let the steam escape (this will help to keep the pastry case crisp).

6. Roughly chop the parsley leaves, then add them to a mixing bowl with the eggs, cream and some salt and pepper and whisk together with a fork.

7. Arrange the garlic evenly over the base of the cooled pastry case, then scatter the potatoes and peas on top. Pour over the egg mixture, then dot the pesto over the top of the filling. Bake the quiche on the hot baking sheet for 25–30 minutes until golden all over and just set in the centre. Serve with mixed salad leaves.

CORNER-SHOP SAMOSAS

If you have a decent corner shop nearby, a quick visit should arm you with everything you need to make these subtly spiced samosas. Feel free to rope in the kids – mine enjoy making them almost as much as they do eating them. And once cooled, they're a fabulous way to jazz up a lunchbox.

MAKES 9 samosas

1 floury potato (about 250g), unpeeled and cut into quarters

1 tablespoon vegetable oil

1 white onion, finely chopped

1 small green chilli, finely chopped

1 tablespoon medium curry powder

2 garlic cloves, crushed

100g paneer cheese, cut into 1cm cubes

75g frozen peas

A handful of coriander, finely chopped

Juice of ½ lemon

6 sheets of filo pastry, defrosted and kept covered with a clean tea towel if frozen

30g unsalted butter, melted

1–2 teaspoons black onion (nigella) seeds

Salt and freshly ground black pepper

1 quantity of Tomato Harissa Sauce (see page 211), to serve

1. Place the potato wedges in a small saucepan of water and bring to the boil, then reduce the heat and simmer for 12–14 minutes until tender. Drain the potato, return to the pan and use a potato masher to mash.

2. Meanwhile, heat the oil in a large frying pan over a medium–high heat. Add the onion, chilli and curry powder and cook over a medium–high heat for about 8 minutes until the onion is soft. Stir through the garlic and cook for a couple of minutes.

3. Add the paneer and peas with a pinch of salt and cook for a further couple of minutes, then stir in the mashed potato, coriander and lemon juice. Season the mixture well with salt and pepper, then remove the pan from the heat and set aside for 5–6 minutes to cool slightly.

4. Preheat the oven to 180°C/160°C fan/Gas Mark 4.

5. Lay a sheet of filo pastry on your work surface and brush with melted butter, then top with a second sheet of filo and again brush with melted butter. Cut your double-thickness filo sheet lengthways into thirds to give you 3 rectangles in total (you want each rectangle to measure about 12 × 36cm.

6. Starting at one end of one filo rectangle, spoon ⅑ of the filling mixture near a corner. Fold the corner with the filling on it diagonally over to form a triangle. Continue to fold in this way down the length of the filo, retaining the triangle shape. Repeat with the remaining filo rectangles. Place the triangles on a cold baking tray, brush with melted butter and sprinkle with black onion seeds.

7. Repeat steps 5 and 6 with the remaining filo sheets and filling until you have 9 triangles.

8. Bake for 20 minutes or until golden and crisp. Serve the samosas hot with the Tomato Harissa Sauce.

SWEETCORN PATTIES WITH AVOCADO SALSA

These patties are brilliant for brunch, best eaten straight from the pan with lashings of the salsa. If you're catering for carnivores, perhaps add some crispy bacon or frizzled chorizo.

MAKES ABOUT 18 patties

1 tablespoon olive oil

1 small bunch of spring onions, finely sliced

2 garlic cloves, finely sliced

1 teaspoon harissa paste

2 courgettes, grated on the largest setting of a box grater

280g sweetcorn kernels, thoroughly defrosted if frozen or thoroughly drained and patted dry if canned

100g plain flour

2 teaspoons baking powder

50g quick-cook polenta

200ml milk

1 red chilli, deseeded and finely chopped, or ½ teaspoon dried chilli flakes

Vegetable oil, for frying

Freshly ground black pepper

For the salsa

2 tomatoes, roughly chopped

½ red onion, finely chopped

1 avocado

Grated zest and juice of 1 unwaxed lime

1 small bunch of coriander, leaves picked and roughly chopped

Salt and freshly ground black pepper

1. Heat the olive oil in a large frying pan, add the spring onions, garlic and harissa paste and cook over a medium heat for 3–4 minutes until the spring onions are completely soft. Tip into a large mixing bowl and add the grated courgettes and sweetcorn. Wipe out the pan with a piece of kitchen paper ready for frying the patties.

2. Sift the flour and baking powder straight on top of the vegetable mixture and then add the polenta. Mix well to evenly coat the veggies in the dry ingredients. Whisk in the milk until a thick batter forms and no patches of flour are visible.

3. Add the chilli and a generous grinding of black pepper and mix to combine. Set aside while you make the salsa.

4. Mix the tomatoes and red onion together in a mixing bowl with a pinch of salt. Halve the avocado and remove the stone, then peel and chop the flesh. Add to the bowl, followed by the lime zest and juice and coriander. Season well with salt and pepper and toss to combine.

5. Heat a couple of tablespoons of vegetable oil in the frying pan over a medium heat. Once the oil is hot, drop a serving spoonful of the batter mixture into the oil and smooth down with the back of the spoon to create a patty about the size of your palm. Repeat with another 2 or 3 spoonfuls of batter, depending on the size of your pan (no more so that you can easily flip them), and fry for 3–4 minutes on each side until crisp and golden. Remove to a plate lined with kitchen paper to absorb the excess oil.

6. Continue frying the remaining batter in batches of 3 or 4 until it is all cooked. The patties should retain the heat quite well, but reheat them in the oven preheated to 180°C/160°C fan/Gas Mark 4 if you'd like them to be piping hot. Serve with the salsa spooned on top.

TIP

IF YOU ARE MAKING THESE FOR YOUNG CHILDREN, YOU MAY WANT TO REDUCE THE QUANTITY OF CHILLI OR LEAVE IT OUT COMPLETELY.

OVEN-ROASTED RATATOUILLE

The traditional French way of making ratatouille, where each vegetable is cooked in separate pans on the hob, is far too faffy for midweek. This throw-it-all-in-the-oven version is not only simpler to make but even more delicious, as the veggies slowly caramelize and become more intense in flavour while roasting.

SERVES 4–6

2 red onions, each cut into 8 wedges

2 aubergines, cut into 2cm cubes

2 red peppers, cored, deseeded and cut into 2cm-wide slices

2 garlic cloves, peeled and bruised with the side of a knife

4 tablespoons olive oil

2 courgettes, quartered lengthways, then cut into 2cm dice

4 tomatoes, roughly chopped

400g can plum tomatoes

1 tablespoon balsamic vinegar

A few sprigs of thyme or oregano

Salt and freshly ground black pepper

1. Preheat the oven to 200°C/180°C fan/Gas Mark 6. Toss the onions, aubergines, peppers and garlic in the olive oil in a large mixing bowl. Divide between 2 deep roasting tins and season well with salt and pepper. Roast for 20 minutes, turning the vegetables twice during this time.

2. Remove the roasting tins from the oven, divide the remaining ingredients between the tins and stir the contents well to evenly combine, using a wooden spoon to break up the tomatoes. Roast for a further 30 minutes, turning the vegetables halfway through this time, or until they are completely soft. Check to make sure they are well seasoned.

Ways to use your ratatouille:

- For a Turkish-inspired supper, add a tablespoon of pomegranate molasses and a 400g can of chickpeas, drained and rinsed, to the roasted vegetables when you add the tomatoes, balsamic and herbs. Serve with couscous or warmed flatbreads.

- For an easy pasta bake, stir the finished ratatouille through cooked pasta along with a dollop of good-quality shop-bought pesto and then pour into a shallow roasting tin. Grate over some Cheddar or Parmesan cheese and bake in the oven at the same temperature as above until the cheese is melted and golden.

- For a satisfying on-the-go snack, stuff the ratatouille into wraps with some grilled halloumi cheese and crisp salad.

- Simply serve the ratatouille with your favourite Higgidy pie.

TIP

IT'S WELL WORTH DOUBLING THE RECIPE AND FREEZING HALF FOR THE FOLLOWING WEEK, AS I OFTEN DO.

SMOKED CHEDDAR TART WITH WALNUT CRUMB

This is the quiche to end all quiches with a combo of crisp walnuts and oozy smoked Cheddar that might be my new favourite. I love this tart simply served with a salad of very finely sliced Granny Smith apple, celery and dill, tossed with a splash of olive oil and cider vinegar.

SERVES 6

EQUIPMENT: 1 × 23cm round loose-bottomed fluted tart tin, 3.5cm deep

1 quantity of Walnutty Pastry (see page 209), or use ready-made shortcrust pastry, defrosted if frozen

A little plain flour, for dusting

For the filling

40g unsalted butter

1 tablespoon olive oil

4 large onions, finely sliced

2 teaspoons light brown soft sugar

1 egg and 2 egg yolks, lightly beaten together

300ml double cream

60g smoked Cheddar cheese, finely grated

1 tablespoon Dijon mustard

¼ teaspoon cayenne pepper

Salt and freshly ground black pepper

For the crumb

25g walnuts, roughly chopped

15g smoked Cheddar cheese, finely grated

15g breadcrumbs (any type)

1. Unless using ready-made pastry, make the Walnutty Pastry according to the method on page 209, then wrap in cling film and leave to rest in the fridge for 30 minutes before using.

2. To make the filling, melt the butter with the olive oil in a large sauté pan. Add the onions, season with salt and pepper and cover the pan with a tight-fitting lid (or foil). Cook over a low heat for 35–40 minutes until soft. Remove the lid (or foil), increase the temperature to medium and cook for a further 10 minutes until the liquid has evaporated. Stir through the sugar and cook for a final 5 minutes until the onions start to turn a light caramel colour. Transfer the onions to a bowl and set aside to cool.

3. Meanwhile, roll the pastry out on a lightly floured surface into a round about 3mm thick and line your tart tin with it, making sure the edges of the pastry stand a little proud above the rim of the tin. Trim the edges to even and prick the base all over with a fork, then chill the pastry case in the fridge for 30 minutes. Don't be tempted to skip this step, as it helps prevent the pastry shrinking when baked.

4. Preheat the oven to 220°C/200°C fan/Gas Mark 7 with a baking sheet inside to heat.

5. Line the pastry case with a piece of non-stick baking paper and fill it with dried beans, uncooked rice or ceramic baking beans. Bake the pastry case for 12 minutes. Remove the paper and baking beans or rice and then bake the pastry case for a further 5 minutes. Remove from the oven and reduce the oven temperature to 180°C/160°C fan/Gas Mark 4.

6. Whisk the whole egg and egg yolk mixture with the cream, Cheddar, mustard and cayenne. Mix the ingredients for the crumb together in a small mixing bowl.

7. Spoon the cooked onions evenly over the base of the pastry case. Pour the egg, cream and cheese mixture over the onions and sprinkle with the crumb mixture. Bake the tart on the hot baking sheet for 30–35 minutes until golden brown and just set. Serve warm.

ONE-PAN BEETROOT & QUINOA SUPPER

If you've never cooked quinoa, perhaps I can persuade you to give it a try. The secret is to toast it in the pan before adding your stock, which lends a wonderful nutty flavour to the finished dish. Beetroot and orange might seem unlikely friends, but the combination of earthiness and fruitiness, together with the crunchy walnuts and salty olives, works a treat.

SERVES 2

150g quinoa, rinsed under cold water and drained

1 tablespoon olive oil

150g raw beetroot, peeled and finely grated

1 small bunch of mint, stalks and leaves separated, stalks finely chopped and leaves reserved for scattering over the quinoa

75g mixed olives, pitted and roughly chopped

500ml vegetable stock

50g walnuts, toasted and roughly chopped

Grated zest of ½ unwaxed orange

To serve

Lemon wedges

Greek yogurt

1. Heat a large frying pan over a medium–low heat, add the rinsed quinoa while it is still wet and toast for about 10 minutes, stirring regularly. At first, the pan will release a lot of steam as the quinoa dries out but continue past this stage until the quinoa grains start popping and smelling nutty. They will also look as though they've puffed up somewhat. It's important to keep a check on the pan and to stir the quinoa regularly to ensure that it toasts evenly and doesn't burn.

2. Add the olive oil, beetroot and mint stalks to the pan and cook, stirring, for 3–4 minutes to remove some of the raw earthiness of the beetroot.

3. Stir in the olives and vegetable stock, bring to the boil and continue boiling, uncovered, for 12–15 minutes until all the liquid has been absorbed.

4. Remove the pan from the heat and leave the quinoa to rest for 5 minutes. Divide between warmed bowls and scatter over the reserved mint leaves, walnuts and orange zest. Serve the quinoa with lemon wedges alongside for squeezing over and a dollop of Greek yogurt.

TIPS

THIS IS A VIBRANT, QUICK DISH THAT I OFTEN MAKE FOR GUESTS WHO CAN'T EAT GLUTEN. FOR A VEGAN VERSION, SIMPLY LEAVE OUT THE GREEK YOGURT.

ONE-PAN PEARL BARLEY & HERB 'RISOTTO'

There's something about the texture of pearl barley that makes this dish a little lighter than a classic rice risotto. But like the traditional version, it does call for regular stirring, which I find strangely therapeutic. The dill, parsley and tarragon add a wonderful freshness, lifting the flavours and lending the finished dish a pretty green hue.

SERVES 3–4

3 tablespoons extra virgin olive oil

2 leeks, trimmed to leave white and light green parts only, cleaned and finely shredded

2 garlic cloves, finely sliced

200g pearl barley

150ml white wine

1.5 litres vegetable stock

100g fresh or frozen peas

1 small bunch of dill, leaves picked and chopped

1 small bunch of flat leaf parsley, leaves picked and chopped

1 small bunch of tarragon, leaves picked and chopped

50g pecorino or Parmesan cheese, grated, plus extra for sprinkling

Grated zest of 1 unwaxed lemon and juice of ½

Salt and freshly ground black pepper

1. Heat 2 tablespoons of the olive oil in a large saucepan, add the leeks and sauté over a low heat, stirring regularly, for 10 minutes until completely soft and translucent.

2. Add the garlic to the pan and cook for a couple of minutes, then stir in the pearl barley until coated in the oil. Cook the pearl barley over a medium heat for a few minutes until it starts to smell nutty. Pour in the white wine and cook, stirring, until completely absorbed. Then add the vegetable stock a ladleful at a time, stirring regularly until each addition has been absorbed before adding the next. Continue cooking the 'risotto' until all the stock is absorbed and the pearl barley is cooked through but retaining a hint of bite.

3. Finally, stir in all the remaining ingredients including the tablespoon of olive oil. Cook for a further minute, then cover the pan with a lid (or foil), remove from the heat and leave the 'risotto' to rest for 5 minutes. Check the seasoning and add salt and pepper to taste before spooning the risotto into warmed bowls and sprinkling with Parmesan.

ROASTED CARROT & CHICKPEA TRAYBAKE

Most of us have roasted a carrot or two in our lifetime, but have you ever tried roasting chickpeas? If not, then you should, as they take on a lovely nutty taste and go deliciously crisp around the edges, providing the perfect foil for soft, sweet roasted carrots as it happens.

SERVES 2 generously

300g small pointy carrots, scrubbed and halved lengthways

4 tablespoons olive oil

1 teaspoon ground coriander

1 teaspoon cumin seeds

1 teaspoon pul biber (Turkish dried chilli flakes), or ½ teaspoon dried chilli flakes

1 orange, halved

400g can chickpeas, drained and dried on kitchen paper

100g peppery salad leaves, such as rocket, watercress or mustard leaves

1 small bunch of dill, leaves picked

Salt and freshly ground black pepper

To serve

1 quantity of Tahini Sauce (see page 211)

100g natural yogurt

Flatbreads or pitta breads

1. Preheat the oven to 200°C/180°C fan/Gas Mark 6. Toss the carrots in a large shallow roasting tin with 2 tablespoons of the olive oil and the spices and season with salt and pepper. Squeeze over the juice of one orange half, then cover the tin tightly with foil and roast for 30 minutes.

2. Remove the tin from the oven, push down on the carrots with a fork to gently crush them and scatter over the chickpeas. Drizzle the remaining olive oil over the top of the chickpeas. The carrots and chickpeas should form a single even layer, but if there is overlap, spread between 2 shallow roasting tins. Roast, uncovered, for a further 25 minutes until the chickpeas start to pop and the carrots are charring at the edges.

3. Remove the tins from the oven, and while the vegetables are still warm, zest about half the remaining orange half over the top and squeeze over all the juice.

4. Transfer the roasted carrots and chickpeas to a large platter and toss with the salad leaves and dill.

5. Mix the Tahini Sauce with the yogurt in a small bowl and drizzle some over the carrot and chickpea mixture, reserving the rest for dipping the flatbreads or pittas into.

TIP

THIS IS A SERIOUSLY HEARTY SUPPER, SO YOU MAY WELL HAVE SOME LEFT OVER, BUT IT'S GREAT FOR LUNCH THE NEXT DAY STUFFED INTO TOASTED PITTA BREADS.

BLACK BEAN CHILLI WITH DIRTY RICE

Dirty rice is a staple of New Orleans cooking – a soul food classic usually made with white rice that has been given a 'dirty' colour thanks to the addition of browned meat, often minced beef and bacon. My veggie version featuring brown rice, Cajun seasoning and the Creole 'Holy Trinity' of spring onion, celery and green pepper sets off my deep, dark black bean chilli perfectly.

SERVES 4

For the dirty rice

300g brown rice

4 tablespoons vegetable oil

1 green pepper, cored, deseeded and finely chopped

2 celery sticks, finely chopped

1 bunch of spring onions, white and green parts peeled and finely sliced

150g frozen peas

1½ tablespoons Cajun seasoning

Pinch of salt

For the black bean chilli

3 tablespoons vegetable oil

1 red onion, finely chopped

2 red peppers, cored, deseeded and diced

4 garlic cloves, finely sliced

1 tablespoon chipotle paste

25g dark chocolate (minimum 90% cocoa solids), finely chopped or grated

400g can chopped tomatoes

400g can black beans, drained

125ml red wine

2 teaspoons clear honey or agave nectar

1 small bunch of coriander, leaves picked and chopped

Grated zest and juice of 1 unwaxed lime

Salt and freshly ground black pepper

Soured cream, to serve

1. First, cook the rice according to the pack instructions, then drain and spread out on a large plate to dry.

2. Next, make a start on the black bean chilli. Heat the vegetable oil in a large saucepan, add the red onion with a pinch of salt and sauté over a medium heat for 7 minutes until soft, sweet and translucent. Add the red peppers, garlic and chipotle paste, reduce the heat and cook for a further 5–6 minutes until the peppers have softened. Stir in the chocolate, tomatoes, beans, red wine and honey or agave nectar. Bring to the boil, then reduce the heat and gently simmer, uncovered, for 25 minutes, stirring occasionally, until the sauce has thickened and turned darker.

3. Meanwhile, to finish the rice, heat the vegetable oil in a large frying pan, add the green pepper and celery and cook over a medium–high heat for a few minutes until they start to soften. Stir in the spring onions and peas, turn the heat up and cook for a minute to soften the peas. Next, add the Cajun seasoning and cook for a couple of minutes until everything is fragrant and the vegetables are soft. Add the salt and the cooked rice and cook for at least 3 minutes, stirring continuously to coat every grain with the vegetables and the spices, until the rice is piping hot.

4. Back to the chilli. Once the sauce has thickened and reduced, remove the pan from the heat and stir in half the coriander and the lime zest and juice. Taste and adjust the seasoning.

5. Divide the rice between warmed bowls and spoon over the chilli. Top each bowl of chilli with a generous spoonful of soured cream and sprinkle over the remaining coriander.

FAST
VEG

When I'm in a real hurry, I look to trusted shortcuts
for a helping hand: some nice artichokes from the
deli counter, a posh pouch of grains. Then I can fling
together a tasty meal in a matter of moments. It may
not be remotely flash, but it will always be delicious.

MOZZARELLA, TOMATO & GREEN OLIVE BREAD SALAD

Like all the best salads, this is a dish of contrasts: the crunch of toasted sourdough set against the creaminess of avocado; the punch of green olives juxtaposed with the sweetness of honey. Make sure you use a good-quality balsamic, as it's thicker and stickier than the standard stuff and has a lovely balance of sharp and sweet.

SERVES 2

2 slices of sourdough bread, roughly torn

100ml olive oil

75g pitted green olives, halved

1 small bunch of mint, leaves picked

50g flaked almonds, toasted

1 teaspoon clear honey

1 avocado, stoned, peeled and sliced

300g mixed tomatoes, smaller ones sliced into halves and larger ones into wedges

125g good-quality mozzarella cheese

1 tablespoon good-quality balsamic vinegar

Salt and freshly ground black pepper

1. Preheat the oven to 220°C/200°C fan/Gas Mark 7. Toss the bread pieces in a shallow roasting tin with 2 tablespoons of the olive oil and sprinkle over a pinch of salt and a grinding of black pepper. Toast the bread for 15 minutes, turning the pieces twice during this time, until it is crisp and golden.

2. Using a food processor or a stick blender, blitz half the olives with three-quarters of the mint, the almonds, honey and the remaining olive oil until you have a chunky sauce.

3. Arrange the avocado, tomatoes and toasted bread on a platter. Tear the mozzarella into pieces and scatter it over the salad, then drizzle over the green olive sauce. Scatter the remaining mint and olives over the top and drizzle with the balsamic vinegar.

ANCIENT GRAIN SALAD WITH SALSA VERDE

If you have a reasonably well-stocked store cupboard and a decent convenience store nearby, you'll be able to rustle up this dish in next to no time. Unlike some salads, it's fabulous the next day, the vibrant Salsa Verde lending it an addictive umami punch.

SERVES 2–3 (with lunchbox leftovers)

1 quantity of Salsa Verde (see page 215)

3 tablespoons olive oil

1 tablespoon lemon juice

1 teaspoon wholegrain mustard

½ teaspoon light brown soft sugar

12 sun-dried tomatoes in oil, drained and roughly chopped

100g fresh or frozen peas

250g pouch ready-cooked mixed grains

100g mixed salad leaves

1. First, make the Salsa Verde according to the method on page 215, then set aside.

2. Whisk the olive oil, lemon juice, mustard and sugar together in a large bowl and toss through the sun-dried tomatoes.

3. Place the peas in a large saucepan and pour boiling water over them, bring to the boil and cook for 1 minute – they should still have a bit of bite to them. Add the mixed grains to the pan to warm through, then drain the whole lot in a sieve.

4. Toss the drained peas and grains in the tomato and dressing mixture. Add the salad leaves and toss to combine.

5. Divide the salad between plates or shallow bowls and spoon the Salsa Verde over the top.

TIP

IF THE MOOD TAKES YOU, TOP THE SALAD WITH SOME GRILLED SLICES OF HALLOUMI CHEESE TO CONTRIBUTE YET MORE HEFT AND ZING.

CHARRED LITTLE GEMS WITH MIXED GRAINS, FALAFEL & TAHINI SAUCE

If the idea of cooking lettuce on a griddle pan seems totally bonkers, all I can say is you must try it. The subtle charring of the Little Gems gives them an alluring smokiness that I love. Shop-bought ready-cooked falafel and grains might seem cheeky, but they are the key to making this impressive-looking lunch so simple to make.

SERVES 2–3

EQUIPMENT: cast-iron griddle pan

100g ready-cooked falafel

2 Little Gem lettuces, halved lengthways

250g pouch ready-cooked mixed grains

1 small bunch of mixed soft herbs (I like mint, flat leaf parsley and coriander), leaves picked and roughly chopped

2 tablespoons olive oil

5 ready-to-eat dried apricots, finely chopped

1 quantity of Tahini Sauce (see page 211)

Salt and freshly ground black pepper

1. Preheat the oven to 220°C/200°C fan/Gas Mark 7. Arrange the falafel on a baking tray and warm through in the oven while you get on with everything else.

2. Heat the griddle pan over a high heat for 5 minutes, then place the lettuce halves, cut side down, on the hot pan. Cook for 3 minutes on each side without moving them to give the char marks a chance to form.

3. Meanwhile, heat the grains according to the pack instructions. Stir through the herbs, olive oil and apricots, then season to taste with salt and pepper.

4. Spoon the grains onto a platter and arrange the charred lettuce over the top. Remove the falafel from the oven and tear them over the lettuce in rough chunks. Spoon some of the Tahini Sauce over the top and serve while the lettuce is still warm.

LEEK & GOATS' CHEESE TRAYBAKE TART

This super-easy tart is really just an exercise in layering. Simply unroll the pastry,
spoon over the pesto and the sautéed leeks and crumble over the goats' cheese,
then bung the tart in the oven. Shop-bought puff pastry is perfect here, but try to find
the all-butter type if you can. I like to eat this with a green salad of peppery leaves
such as watercress and rocket tossed in a mustardy dressing.

SERVES 4

EQUIPMENT: 1 baking tray,
about 20 × 30cm

320g sheet of ready-rolled
all-butter puff pastry, defrosted
if frozen

A little plain flour, for dusting,
if needed

30g unsalted butter

2 tablespoons olive oil

2 large leeks, trimmed, cleaned
and very finely shredded (the
finer the shredding, the faster
the leeks will cook)

3 tablespoons water

100g good-quality shop-bought
pesto

125g soft goats' cheese

A few sprigs of thyme, leaves
picked

1 beaten egg, to glaze

Freshly ground black pepper

1. Preheat the oven to 200°C/180°C fan/Gas Mark 6 with a baking sheet inside to heat.

2. Line your baking tray with non-stick baking paper. Unroll the sheet of puff pastry and use it to line the tray – roll it out a little on a lightly floured surface if necessary so that the edges of the pastry just come up the sides of the tray. Pop the tray in the fridge for 15 minutes.

3. Melt the butter with the oil in a large frying pan, and when it's foaming, add the shredded leeks and measured water. Cover the pan with a lid and cook over a medium heat for 10–12 minutes. Remove the lid and cook for a further 5 minutes or until the leeks are completely soft and translucent and have reduced in volume by one-third. Remove the pan from the heat and set aside to cool for a moment.

4. Remove the pastry case from the fridge and spread the pesto over the base, leaving a 1cm border all round. Carefully spoon the leek mixture evenly on top of the pesto. Crumble over the goats' cheese, sprinkle over the thyme leaves and add a grinding of black pepper.

5. Using kitchen scissors, carefully make an angled snip in the pastry from each corner inwards, then carefully fold the pastry edges inwards a little to create a slightly raised border. Brush all the pastry edges with beaten egg to glaze. Bake the tart on the hot baking sheet for 25–30 minutes until the leeks are catching in places and the cheese is golden in colour.

6. Remove the tart from the oven and leave to cool slightly before sliding it out of the tray. Cut the tart into 4 large rectangles and serve hot or warm.

TIP

BAKING THE TART ON A HOT BAKING SHEET HELPS ENSURE THAT THE PASTRY COOKS
FROM UNDERNEATH.

ARTICHOKE & BUTTER BEAN SALAD

I've become mildly obsessed with those tall jars of butter beans you sometimes see now. I'm not entirely sure about the science behind it, but they're so much softer and more buttery than the canned type. If, however, you struggle to track them down, fret not, as the ones in cans will still do the job admirably.

SERVES 4

2 tablespoons olive oil

2 garlic cloves, finely sliced

600g jar butter beans, drained and a little liquid from the jar reserved

Grated zest and juice of 1 unwaxed lemon

15 sun-dried tomatoes in oil, drained and roughly chopped, 2 tablespoons of the oil from the jar reserved

175g pack grilled artichokes (available from most deli counters)

3 tablespoons flat leaf parsley, roughly chopped

1–2 tablespoons sherry vinegar

Salt and freshly ground black pepper

1. Heat the olive oil in a large frying pan, add the garlic and sauté over a medium heat for a minute or so. Stir in the butter beans with the reserved liquid from the jar and half the lemon zest and all the juice. Cook for a couple of minutes or until the beans have warmed through.

2. Stir through the sun-dried tomatoes with the reserved oil from the jar and the artichokes. Season with salt and pepper.

3. Spoon the bean and tomato mixture into a bowl and add the chopped parsley. Toss to combine and coat with the flavours from the pan.

4. Divide the salad between 4 shallow bowls, drizzle the sherry vinegar over the top and decorate with the remaining grated lemon zest.

CAULIFLOWER COUSCOUS

It's not particularly hard to make your own cauliflower 'couscous', but if you're in a mad rush to get something tasty on the table, I see nothing wrong in using the ready-made stuff. You can usually find it in the supermarket alongside the other prepared veg. The only non-negotiable factor here is that you must sauté it before mixing it with the other ingredients, whereby it will take on an irresistible nutty flavour.

SERVES 4

2 tablespoons olive oil

2 × 300g packs cauliflower couscous (sometimes called 'cauliflower rice')

1 teaspoon ground cumin

½ teaspoon ground cinnamon

75g mixed seeds, toasted (I use pumpkin and sunflower)

Grated zest and juice of 1 unwaxed lemon, or more juice to taste

50g feta cheese, crumbled

50g golden sultanas or raisins

1 small bunch of mixed soft herbs (I like dill, basil, flat leaf parsley and mint, but one type will do if that's all you have), leaves picked and chopped

Salt and freshly ground black pepper

1. Heat half the olive oil in a large frying pan, and add half the cauliflower couscous with a pinch of salt and pepper and cook over a high heat, stirring regularly with a wooden spoon, for a couple of minutes until charred in places and tasting nutty. Tip into a large bowl. Repeat with the remaining oil and couscous.

2. Wipe out the pan with a piece of kitchen paper, then toast the spices over a medium heat without any oil until they release their fragrance – this will only take about 15 seconds. Stir the spices through the cauliflower couscous.

3. Add the seeds, lemon zest and juice, feta, sultanas or raisins and all but a handful of the herbs. Check the seasoning and add more salt, pepper and/or lemon juice to taste.

4. Arrange the couscous on a platter and scatter the remaining herbs over the top.

BROCCOLI WITH SESAME NOODLES & STICKY PRESERVED LEMONS

You might normally associate preserved lemons with North African cooking, such as heady tagines and gutsy Moroccan salads. But their complex salty zing can bring a welcome zip to all sorts of dishes, and they work particularly well chopped up in a stir-fry. Griddled broccoli is a wonderful discovery too. If you've tried neither, now might be just the time.

SERVES 2

200g Tenderstem broccoli, cut into 3cm pieces

4 tablespoons olive oil

2 garlic cloves, finely sliced

½ preserved lemon, flesh and pith discarded, rind finely chopped

50g white sesame seeds

2 tablespoons soy sauce

300g pack ready-cooked fine rice noodles

Salt and freshly ground black pepper

1. Preheat the grill on its highest setting.

2. Meanwhile, add the broccoli to a roasting tin, drizzle over a tablespoon of the olive oil and season with salt and pepper. Rub the broccoli all over with the oil and seasoning so that the pieces are evenly coated.

3. Place the tin under the hot grill for 5–7 minutes, tossing the broccoli pieces once or twice during this time, until they are crisp at the ends and charred in places.

4. While the broccoli is grilling, heat the remaining 3 tablespoons of olive oil in a frying pan large enough to accommodate the noodles. Add the garlic and sauté for a minute until it begins to take on the faintest colour, but not so much that it starts to brown. Add the preserved lemon and cook, stirring, for a minute until it starts to release its fragrance. Remove the pan from the heat and add the sesame seeds, which will pop and jump out of the pan initially, but they'll soon settle down.

5. Use tongs to toss the soy sauce and noodles through the preserved lemon and garlic-flavoured oil. Finally, toss the grilled broccoli through the noodles, then divide between 2 warmed bowls and serve.

20-MINUTE FRIDGE TO FRITTATA

Simple doesn't have to mean subtle. There is nothing wrong with light, elegant dishes, but my passion is, and probably always will be, for big, bold, punchy flavours. And this frittata, though pretty straightforward (it has just seven ingredients), is certainly not shy. Sliced into fat wedges and served warm or cold, it makes a truly tasty brunch or lunch.

SERVES 6

EQUIPMENT: 1 × 26cm ovenproof non-stick frying pan

300g mixed mushrooms, such as chestnut, shiitake, oyster and/or enoki

2 tablespoons olive oil, plus extra for brushing

2 garlic cloves, roughly chopped

8 large eggs

6 spring onions, sliced

3 tablespoons roughly chopped herbs (I like curly parsley, tarragon, chives, dill or coriander)

40g Parmesan or pecorino cheese, grated

Salt and freshly ground black pepper

1. Trim and thickly slice the chestnut mushrooms, gently tear the shiitake and oyster mushrooms depending on their size and, if using, divide the enoki mushrooms.

2. Heat the olive oil in the ovenproof frying pan, add the garlic and sauté over a medium heat for 1 minute. Add the prepared mushrooms and cook over a high heat for 6–7 minutes until they are golden and slightly crispy and have finished releasing their liquid. Season the mushrooms with a good grinding of black pepper, then remove them from the pan and set aside.

3. Crack the eggs into a large mixing bowl and use a fork to whisk together with the spring onions, herbs and half the cheese. Season well with salt and pepper.

4. Using a pastry brush or kitchen paper, coat the whole frying pan – still warm from frying the mushrooms – with olive oil, ensuring that the sides are well greased. Set the pan over a medium heat before pouring in the herby egg mixture. Scatter over the fried mushrooms and spread them evenly, pushing some into the egg mixture but leaving others to protrude above the surface of the egg.

5. Preheat the grill on a medium–high setting.

6. Meanwhile, gently cook the egg mixture on the hob for about 9–10 minutes until the base is firm and the egg is cooked about 1cm in from the edges but the centre is still a little wobbly. Sprinkle over the remaining cheese.

7. Place the pan under the grill and cook the frittata for about a minute until the top is golden and puffed. Be careful not to overcook the frittata, as it will continue to cook in the residual heat. Remove the pan from the grill and leave to cool for a few minutes.

8. Place a large, flat plate over the top of the pan and hold it in place as you invert the pan and plate together as quickly as possible so that the frittata falls onto the plate, then lift the pan away. Flip the frittata back onto its base before serving.

BRAISED ROOTS WITH ORZO

Despite the addition of orzo, a rice-shaped pasta popular in Italy and Greece, this simple braise feels oddly British but in a good way. It's cosy and soothing, and therefore perfect for a cold, midwinter evening. To me, it seems like a cleaner, more saintly version of a classic hotpot, and not only is it meat-free but quite by accident it's vegan too.

SERVES 4–6

100ml olive oil

1kg aromatic root vegetables (I like swede, carrot, celeriac and parsnips), peeled and cut into irregular-shaped 2cm pieces

4 garlic cloves, finely sliced

2 bay leaves

2 teaspoons fennel seeds

2 teaspoons dried marjoram or oregano

Grated zest and juice of 2 unwaxed lemons

200g dried orzo

1 small bunch of mint, leaves picked

Salt and freshly ground black pepper

1. Heat the olive oil gently in a large, heavy-based saucepan. Add all the root veg with 1 teaspoon of salt and stir to coat the vegetables in the oil. Cook over a medium heat, stirring occasionally, for 15 minutes until the vegetables are starting to take on some golden colour.

2. Stir in the garlic, bay leaves, fennel seeds and marjoram or oregano and the lemon juice. Fill a kettle with water and bring to the boil, then pour 100ml of the boiling water into the pan, cover the pan with a lid and cook over a medium heat for 20 minutes until the vegetables are completely soft.

3. Stir through the orzo and pour over 1 litre of hot water from the kettle. Cover the pan again and cook over a medium heat for 10 minutes until the orzo is cooked through. Meanwhile, finely chop the mint, reserving a few smaller leaves for garnish.

4. Once the orzo is done, stir through the chopped mint and lemon zest. Taste and adjust the seasoning, adding more salt and some pepper if you like.

5. Spoon the slightly soupy root veg mixture into warmed bowls and top with the reserved mint leaves.

20-MINUTE PANTRY-TO-PLATE PAPPARDELLE

For such a quick and easy recipe, this is a riot of tastes and textures. With its soft ribbons of pasta, crunchy toasted pistachios, sweet green peas and nutty Parmesan, it's a real delight. Install yourselves in front of the TV, grab a bowl of this and a fork each and away you go.

SERVES 4

150g frozen peas

250g dried pappardelle pasta

100g raw pistachio nuts, toasted

60g basil

50g Parmesan cheese, grated, plus extra to serve

1 tablespoon apple cider vinegar

1 teaspoon clear honey or agave syrup

4 tablespoons olive oil

Grated zest and juice of 1 unwaxed lemon

Salt and freshly ground black pepper

1. Bring a large saucepan of well-salted water to the boil. Add the peas and boil for 1 minute or until they rise to the surface. Using a sieve, scoop the peas out of the pan, shaking off the excess water as you go, and add all but a handful to a food processor.

2. Add the pappardelle to the pea cooking water and cook according to the pack instructions.

3. While the pasta is cooking, add three-quarters of the pistachios, the basil, Parmesan, vinegar, honey or agave syrup and olive oil to the food processor and blitz until you have a chunky pesto. Check the seasoning and add salt and pepper to taste.

4. Scoop out a mugful of the pasta cooking water before draining the pasta in a colander, then return the pasta to the pan with the reserved cooking water and peas and all the pesto. Use tongs to turn the pasta in the pesto and to create a sauce with the pasta cooking water and pesto. Roughly chop the remaining pistachios.

5. Divide the pasta between 4 warmed bowls and top with the chopped pistachios and lemon zest and juice. Grate over some extra Parmesan and serve immediately.

PICKLED CUCUMBER & SMOKED TOFU GLASS NOODLE SALAD

On its lonesome, tofu doesn't have a huge amount of character, but that's what makes it such a valuable ingredient – it's a fabulous absorber of flavours, in this case ginger, chilli and soy sauce. Buying ready-cooked rice noodles makes this salad very quick to put together.

SERVES 4

For the quick-pickled cucumber

½ cucumber, cut into ribbons with a Y-shaped vegetable peeler

Grated zest and juice of 1 unwaxed lime

2 tablespoons rice vinegar

1 teaspoon light muscovado sugar

1 teaspoon salt

For the tofu

1 small thumb of fresh root ginger, peeled and finely grated

1 red chilli, deseeded and finely chopped

1 garlic clove, finely chopped

2 teaspoons clear honey or maple syrup

4 tablespoons soy sauce

4 tablespoons sunflower oil

3 tablespoons cornflour

200g smoked tofu, dried between sheets of kitchen paper and cut into 2cm cubes

Grated zest and juice of 1 unwaxed lime

For the salad

50g raw cashew nuts, toasted and roughly chopped

200g pack ready-cooked vermicelli rice noodles

1 small bunch of coriander, leaves picked

1 small bunch of mint, leaves picked

1. First, pickle the cucumber. Toss the cucumber ribbons with the other pickling ingredients in a non-metallic mixing bowl. Place a saucer over the top of the cucumber and weigh down with a food can or jar. Set aside while you prepare the rest of the salad.

2. For the tofu, mix the ginger, chilli, garlic, honey or maple syrup, soy and 2 tablespoons of the sunflower oil together in a small bowl and set aside. Scatter the cornflour over a plate and roll the tofu cubes in the cornflour to coat each side (you may not need it all).

3. Heat the remaining 2 tablespoons of sunflower oil in a large frying pan, add the tofu and cook over a medium heat, stirring regularly with a wooden spoon, until it's crisp and golden all over. Turn up the heat, pour in half the soy mixture (you'll use the remainder as a dressing later) and cook, stirring continuously, for 30 seconds or until the mixture has thickened. Remove the pan from the heat and stir in the lime zest and juice.

4. To assemble the salad, toss the cucumber, cashews and cooked tofu in a large salad bowl with the remaining soy mixture, noodles and coriander and mint leaves.

TIP

THIS ZINGY, ASIAN-INSPIRED SALAD IS LOVELY IN A LUNCHBOX.

BROAD BEAN & CHIVE GNOCCHI

People seem a little fearful of gnocchi, and the idea of making your own can understandably be intimidating. But since so many Italians buy theirs ready-made from the supermarket, I see no shame in following suit. This recipe features one of my top tips for adding textural interest to a dish: blitzing half the beans and leaving half whole. The munchiness of the whole broad beans against the creaminess of the blended ones is a real treat.

SERVES 4

500g pack ready-made potato gnocchi

400g can broad beans, drained

½ small bunch of chives, snipped

½ small bunch of flat leaf parsley, finely chopped

100ml crème fraîche

Grated zest and juice of 1 unwaxed lemon

100g Parmesan cheese, grated

Salt and freshly ground black pepper

1. Bring a large saucepan of salted water to the boil. Add the gnocchi and cook according to the pack instructions.

2. Add half the broad beans to a food processor along with a handful of the herbs (reserving the remainder for adding later), the crème fraîche, lemon juice and a splash of the gnocchi cooking water. Blitz until smooth.

3. Drain the gnocchi and return it to the pan. Stir the broad bean sauce through, then add the remaining whole broad beans and herbs and season with salt and pepper.

4. Divide the gnocchi between 4 warmed bowls and sprinkle the lemon zest and Parmesan over the top.

SPRING VEG WITH ROASTED FETA

Every now and then I make a culinary discovery and it's everything I could wish for all at once.
One such revelation is roasted feta, so promise me you'll try this recipe.

SERVES 4

EQUIPMENT: 3 large shallow roasting tins

1 red onion, cut into 8 wedges

250g asparagus spears, woody ends snapped off (see tip)

150g mangetout

150g small green peppers (padron peppers work well)

150g radishes

400g can artichoke hearts, drained and halved

1 fennel bulb, trimmed and cut into 8 wedges

1 small bunch of spring onions, trimmed

1 lemon, halved

Extra virgin olive oil, for drizzling

1 tablespoon pul biber (Turkish dried chilli flakes), or 1½ teaspoons dried chilli flakes

200g feta cheese

400g can butter beans or cannellini beans, drained

1 teaspoon za'atar

Salt and freshly ground black pepper

For the dressing

1 bunch of mixed soft herbs (I like mint, flat leaf parsley and dill), leaves picked

4 tablespoons extra virgin olive oil

1 tablespoon white wine vinegar

2 teaspoons clear honey

1. Preheat the oven to 220°C/200°C fan/Gas Mark 7.

2. Divide all the vegetables between 2 large shallow roasting tins. Place a lemon half in the centre of each tin and drizzle enough olive oil over the vegetables to coat. Season generously with salt and pepper and sprinkle the chilli flakes evenly over the vegetables.

3. Place the feta in the centre of a separate shallow roasting tin and tumble the butter or cannellini beans around the cheese. Sprinkle over the za'atar and drizzle over some olive oil.

4. Place the vegetable tins on the top 2 shelves of the oven with the feta and beans underneath. Roast for 30 minutes until everything is softened and catching in places, turning the vegetables twice during this time.

5. While the vegetables are roasting, make the dressing. Finely chop the herb leaves and then whisk with the oil, vinegar and honey in a small bowl.

6. Remove the tins from the oven and leave all the ingredients to cool for 5 minutes before squeezing over the juice from the roasted lemon halves – they may still be very hot, so use tongs to hold them and squeeze the juice out with a fork.

7. Arrange the roasted vegetables on a platter and break the roasted feta over the top. Scatter over the beans, which should have popped and crisped up in the oven, then drizzle the dressing over everything.

TIP

ASPARAGUS SPEARS HAVE A NATURAL BREAKING POINT JUST ABOVE WHERE THE TENDER STEM BECOMES WOODY. TO REMOVE THE WOODY END, HOLD THE STEM OF THE ASPARAGUS SPEAR WITH BOTH HANDS AND BEND IT NEAR THE BASE UNTIL THE STEM SNAPS.

VERY GREEN FRITTERS

The beauty of this recipe is its flexibility, so don't feel you need to follow the instructions slavishly – it can be just as delicious made with whatever you happen to have lurking in your fridge or freezer. No courgettes? Frozen peas will work wonderfully instead. Out of spinach? Try using some rocket. And crumbly feta makes a fab alternative to the soft goats' cheese. I like to eat these fritters with oven-roasted baby tomatoes and warm flatbreads.

MAKES 8 fritters

2 tablespoons plain flour

200g courgettes, grated or spiralized

2 handfuls of baby spinach, washed and dried

1 small bunch of chives, very finely chopped

2 large eggs, beaten

30g Parmesan cheese, grated

100g soft goats' cheese

A knob of unsalted butter and a glug of oil, for frying

Salt and freshly ground black pepper

1. Measure the flour into a mixing bowl, add the courgettes and toss them around to coat them in the flour. Add the spinach and chives and toss again to evenly distribute the veg.

2. Pour in the beaten eggs, season generously with salt and pepper and stir well. Add the Parmesan and crumble in the goats' cheese, then stir again to combine.

3. Set a large frying pan over a medium heat and add the butter and oil. Once the fat is hot, carefully add dollops of the fritter mixture to the pan and cook for a couple of minutes, then flip over and cook for a further 2 minutes. Serve immediately.

TIP

USE POTATO FLOUR IN PLACE OF PLAIN FLOUR FOR A GLUTEN-FREE OPTION.

VEG
FEASTS

As much as I love simple cooking, sometimes it's fun to pull out all the stops and create a real showstopper. Yes, these recipes take a little more effort, but if you have the time and you're in the mood, you'll be richly rewarded. As will your guests.

TOMATO & TARRAGON TARTE TATIN

Serving a tarte tatin is a 'tah-dah!' moment, as they always look stunning, and this sweet and savoury version is no exception. It's a celebration of the tomato, and the more types you use – large and small, red and yellow – the more interesting the dish will be. And there's no need to limit yourself to just-picked, perfect fruits; some overripe toms will make for an even tastier tart.

SERVES 6

EQUIPMENT: 1 × 28cm
ovenproof non-stick
frying pan

For the tarte tatin

1.25kg mixed tomatoes, all
shapes, colours and sizes

Extra virgin olive oil,
for cooking

1 small bunch of spring
onions, finely sliced

2 garlic cloves, finely sliced

150g spinach, washed

¾ bunch of tarragon,
leaves picked

320g sheet of ready-rolled
all-butter puff pastry,
defrosted if frozen

A little plain flour,
for dusting

Salt and freshly ground
black pepper

**For the tarragon
mascarpone**

250g mascarpone cheese

¼ bunch of tarragon,
leaves picked

Salt and freshly ground
black pepper

1. Preheat the oven to 120°C/100°C fan/Gas Mark ½. Halve the tomatoes around their middles and arrange, cut side up, in 2 shallow roasting tins. Sprinkle over a generous pinch of salt and grind over some black pepper. Bake on the middle shelf of the oven for 1½–2 hours, but keep an eye on the smaller tomatoes, as they'll cook much more quickly. Open the oven door from time to time to release some steam. The tomatoes are done when their skins are blistered but not burned.

2. Meanwhile, warm a splash of olive oil in the ovenproof frying pan over a medium heat, add the spring onions and garlic and cook until they start to take on some golden colour. Add the spinach with a pinch of salt and keep stirring the spinach until it's completely wilted, then remove the pan from the heat. Transfer the spinach to a sieve over the sink and press with the back of a wooden spoon to squeeze out as much moisture as you can. Set aside.

3. When the tomatoes are ready, remove them from the oven and turn the oven up to 180°C/160°C fan/Gas Mark 4. Wipe the frying pan with kitchen paper and drizzle the base with 2 tablespoons of olive oil. Place the tomatoes, cut side down, on the pan base, nestling the tarragon leaves among them as you go. Spread the spinach evenly over the top of the tomatoes.

4. Roll the sheet of puff pastry out on a lightly floured surface so that it's slightly larger than your pan. Lay the puff pastry over the top of the spinach and use a sharp knife to trim the edges around the pan, then tuck the pastry edges down around the sides of the pan on the inside. Bake for 25 minutes until the pastry has puffed up and the top is deep golden in colour.

5. Meanwhile, whip the mascarpone in a mixing bowl with an electric whisk until it's light and airy, then roughly chop the tarragon leaves and fold them through. Season to taste with salt and pepper.

6. Remove the tart from the oven and let it cool for 10 minutes before running a spatula around the side to loosen. Place a larger, flat plate or board over the top of the pan and hold it in place as you invert the pan and plate together. Tap the base of the pan to loosen the tart so that it falls onto the plate or board, then lift the pan away. Serve with the tarragon mascarpone for spooning over.

FENNEL & GREEN OLIVE LASAGNE

This is one seriously chic lasagne. All the flavours here are very grown-up indeed: fennel, sherry, olives and tarragon. And, perhaps surprisingly, there are no tomatoes. My kids wouldn't be overly impressed, but then this is much more of an entertaining lasagne than an everyday one. It requires a certain amount of effort, but your foodie friends will repay you in compliments.

SERVES 6

EQUIPMENT: 1 × 24cm square ovenproof dish or roasting tin

2 tablespoons olive oil

3 white onions, finely sliced

3 fennel bulbs, trimmed and finely sliced

2 garlic cloves, finely sliced

125ml dry sherry

100g curly kale, washed and tough stalks removed

100g green olives, pitted and roughly chopped

50g unsalted butter, plus a little extra for greasing

50g plain flour

500ml milk

200ml vegetable stock

⅛ whole nutmeg, grated

250g ricotta cheese

50g Parmesan cheese, grated

1 egg, lightly beaten

½ teaspoon dried oregano

½ small bunch of tarragon, leaves picked and roughly chopped

150g dried lasagne sheets

Salt and freshly ground black pepper

1. Heat the olive oil in a large frying pan over a low heat, add the onions, fennel and garlic with a pinch of salt and cook slowly, stirring regularly, for 30 minutes until the vegetables are caramelized and have reduced by half in volume.

2. Turn the heat up to medium, pour in the sherry and cook, stirring regularly, until all the liquid has been absorbed and the vegetables look jammy.

3. Preheat the oven to 200°C/180°C fan/Gas Mark 6.

4. Place the kale in a large sieve or colander. Fill a kettle with water and bring to the boil, then pour the boiling water over the kale and leave to cool for a couple of minutes before squeezing out as much liquid as you can with your hands. Add the kale to the fennel mixture along with the olives. Remove the pan from the heat.

5. Melt the butter in a medium saucepan until it starts to bubble and stir in the flour with a wooden spoon. Cook over a medium heat for about a minute, stirring regularly, until the mixture has turned a shade darker and smells toasty. Gradually add the milk and vegetable stock and whisk continuously until the sauce has thickened and coats the back of the spoon. Remove the pan from the heat and season the sauce with the nutmeg and salt and pepper to taste.

6. Whisk the ricotta, all but a handful of the Parmesan, the beaten egg, oregano and all but a sprinkling of the tarragon together with a fork in a bowl. Set aside.

7. Lightly grease the ovenproof dish or roasting tin with butter. Arrange half of the vegetable mixture evenly over the base of the dish or tin. Top with half the lasagne sheets, then dot over half the ricotta mixture and pour over half the white sauce. Repeat with the remaining ingredients, finishing with the ricotta mixture and white sauce. Sprinkle over the remaining Parmesan and chopped tarragon.

8. Bake for 40 minutes until the top is bubbling and golden. Serve hot.

STUFFED BULGUR AUBERGINE WITH CHERMOULA

This dish is the modern, Middle Eastern equivalent of the filled jacket potato, using velvety, soft aubergines instead of spuds. If the chermoula topping seems a bit of a stretch, use a good-quality jarred version instead – you'll find it in most supermarkets next to the harissa paste.

SERVES 4

4 aubergines
3–4 tablespoons good-quality olive oil
Juice of 1 lemon
Pinch of sea salt
Freshly ground black pepper

For the bulgur salad
1 tablespoon olive oil
1 large red onion or 2 small, finely sliced
4 garlic cloves, thinly sliced
1 teaspoon paprika
450ml vegetable stock
150g bulgur wheat
3 tablespoons chopped flat leaf parsley

For the chermoula
1 teaspoon cumin seeds
½ teaspoon coriander seeds
15g coriander, roughly chopped
15g flat leaf parsley, roughly chopped
2 garlic cloves, crushed
½ red chilli, deseeded and finely chopped
Grated zest and juice of 1 unwaxed lemon
1 teaspoon smoked paprika
100ml olive oil
¼ teaspoon salt, or more to taste if needed
Freshly ground black pepper

1. First, make the bulgur salad. Heat a large frying pan over a high heat and add the olive oil. Once the oil is hot, add the onion and cook for 1–2 minutes, then stir in the garlic and paprika.

2. Bring the vegetable stock to a simmer in a small saucepan over a medium heat. Add the bulgur wheat and gently cook for 8–10 minutes until the grains have plumped up and are cooked through. Remove from the heat and stir through the red onion mixture and parsley. Set aside.

3. Meanwhile, make the chermoula. Heat a small, dry frying pan over a medium heat, add the cumin and coriander seeds and cook for 2 minutes until just toasted. Transfer to a small mixing bowl, add the remaining chermoula ingredients and mix to combine. Season to taste, then set aside.

4. Preheat the oven to its hottest setting and, once it is roasting hot, turn it to the grill setting. Pierce each aubergine twice with a small, sharp knife. Place on a baking sheet under the grill, with the oven door closed, for 25 minutes or until the aubergine skin is black and the flesh is collapsed and soft, using tongs to turn halfway through this time. Remove from the oven, then slice each hot aubergine lengthways down the centre, being careful not to cut all the way through, and split open. Drizzle with the olive oil and lemon juice, and season with the sea salt and some pepper.

5. Serve the aubergines heaped with a spoonful of the bulgur wheat salad and a spoonful of chermoula.

TIP

FOR A MEZZE-STYLE MEAL, THIS IS GREAT SERVED ALONGSIDE A COUPLE OF DIPS – TRY THE BEETROOT MUHAMMARA OR THE RED PEPPER ROMESCO – AND SOME QUICK YOGURT FLATBREADS (SEE PAGES 163–6).

RAW SUMMER VEGETABLE TART

The secret to this dish is crisp homemade pastry, a smooth avocado and mascarpone layer and a fresh, zingy topping made with ribbons of courgette dressed with lemon, olive oil and sweet green herbs. Summer on a plate.

SERVES 6

EQUIPMENT: 1 rectangular loose-bottomed fluted tart tin, 20 × 30cm; a Y-shaped vegetable peeler

1 quantity of Savoury Shortcrust Pastry (see page 206), or use ready-made shortcrust pastry, defrosted if frozen

A little plain flour, for dusting

For the filling

2 small ripe avocados

250g mascarpone cheese

50g fresh or dried white breadcrumbs

1 garlic clove, crushed

30g Parmesan cheese, finely grated

A small handful of basil leaves

For the topping

2 courgettes

A handful of mixed soft herbs (such as basil, coriander, dill and flat leaf parsley)

Grated zest and juice of 1 unwaxed lemon

1 tablespoon extra virgin olive oil

Salt and freshly ground black pepper

1. Unless using ready-made pastry, make the Savoury Shortcrust Pastry according to the method on page 206, then wrap in cling film and leave to rest in the fridge for 30 minutes.

2. Preheat the oven to 200°C/180°C fan/Gas Mark 6.

3. Roll the pastry out on a lightly floured surface into a thin, even rectangle large enough to line the tart tin. Lift the pastry by rolling it around a rolling pin and then unrolling it over the tin. Don't worry if the pastry cracks – just use your fingers to patch the pieces together. Ease the pastry into the corners of the tin, then use the rolling pin to roll firmly across the top of the tin to trim away any excess pastry. Chill in the fridge for 30 minutes.

4. Line the pastry case with a piece of non-stick baking paper and fill it with dried beans, uncooked rice or ceramic baking beans. Bake the pastry case in the top third of the oven for 25 minutes or until the visible pastry is sandy coloured. Remove the paper and baking beans or rice and then bake the pastry case for a further 10–12 minutes to ensure that the base is cooked. Remove from the oven and set aside to cool.

5. Meanwhile, make the filling. Halve the avocados and remove the stones, then scoop out the avocado flesh into a food processor. Add the remaining filling ingredients and blitz until smooth. Spoon the mixture into the cooled pastry case.

6. Finish the tart with the fresh vegetable topping. Using a Y-shaped vegetable peeler, peel thin strips of courgette into a large mixing bowl, discarding the white fleshy core. Pick the leaves from the herb stalks and add to the bowl along with the lemon zest and juice, olive oil and plenty of seasoning. Mix to combine, then arrange on top of the avocado filling. Cut the tart into squares to serve.

WHOLE ROASTED COCONUT CAULIFLOWER WITH CRISPY POTATOES & GREENS

If there's a more dramatic veggie centrepiece than this, I have yet to find it. But don't be put off by the long list of ingredients – you will be rewarded for your efforts with a chorus of wows as you bring it to the table. And as it's a one-tray meal, you won't have to bother with side dishes. Some accompanying shop-bought naan and Indian chutney will more than suffice.

SERVES 6

For the coconut paste

4 spring onions, roughly chopped

1 green chilli, deseeded and roughly chopped

1 small bunch of coriander, stalks and leaves separated, leaves reserved for scattering over the cauliflower, stalks roughly chopped

garlic cloves, peeled and roughly chopped

1 small thumb of fresh root ginger, peeled and roughly chopped

2 teaspoons ground turmeric or 1 small thumb of fresh turmeric, peeled and roughly chopped

1 tablespoon cumin seeds, toasted

1 tablespoon coriander seeds, toasted

400ml can coconut milk

Continued overleaf >>

1. Preheat the oven to 200°C/180°C fan/Gas Mark 6.

2. First, make the coconut paste. Using a food processor or stick blender, blitz the spring onions, green chilli, coriander stalks, garlic, ginger, turmeric and cumin and coriander seeds with half the can of coconut milk until a rough paste forms.

3. Bring a large saucepan of water to the boil, lower in the potatoes and boil for 15 minutes or until a sharp knife passes through them easily. Drain and set aside.

4. Place the cauliflower in a deep roasting tin and pour the remaining coconut milk around it. Scatter the kaffir lime leaves over the coconut milk. Rub 1 tablespoon of the coconut oil over the cauliflower and season well with salt and pepper. Then use a spatula or spoon to rub the spice paste all over the cauliflower, getting into every crevice of each floret. Squeeze the lime juice over the cauliflower. Cover the tin tightly with foil, place on the middle shelf of the oven and roast the cauliflower for 20 minutes.

5. Meanwhile, heat the remaining 3 tablespoons of coconut oil in a separate shallow roasting tin on the top shelf of the oven above the cauliflower for a couple of minutes. Carefully remove the tin from the oven, arrange the potatoes in a single even layer in the hot oil and use a potato masher to press down on them just to split their skins. Scatter the mustard and coriander seeds over the top, season well with salt and pepper and roast on the top shelf for 45 minutes until the potatoes are crispy and golden all over.

Continued overleaf >>

For the coconut cauliflower

500g baby potatoes, larger ones halved

1 large cauliflower (about 750g)

4 kaffir lime leaves

4 tablespoons coconut oil

Juice of 1 lime

2 teaspoons mustard seeds, bashed with a pestle and mortar or rolling pin

1 teaspoon coriander seeds, bashed with a pestle and mortar or rolling pin

100g curly kale, washed and tough stalks removed

2 red chillies, deseeded and finely chopped, plus 1 extra, cut into slivers, for garnish (but this is optional!)

Salt and freshly ground black pepper

6. Once the cauliflower has roasted for 20 minutes, lift the foil away and baste the top with the bubbling, spiced coconut milk from the tin. Roast, uncovered, for a further 25–30 minutes until the top of the cauliflower is crispy and charring.

7. When the roasted potatoes are done, remove the tin from the oven, scatter the kale and chopped red chillies over the potatoes and stir to coat in the flavoured oil. Roast for 5 minutes until the kale is just starting to wilt but is still bright green.

8. Lift the kale and potatoes out of the tin with a slotted spoon and arrange on a large platter. Place the cauliflower in the centre of the platter and spoon over any bright yellow liquid from the tin. Scatter over the reserved coriander leaves. At the table, use a serrated knife to slice the cauliflower into bold wedges and, if you want extra heat, garnish with the slivers of bright red chilli.

MISO SQUASH & CHARD PIE

Boxing Day lunch can be tricky. Because Christmas dinner sets the bar so high, it's easy
to find yourself wondering 'How do I top that?' The answer is with this pie. Not only does
it look suitably dramatic, but it delivers the sort of bold, gutsy flavours that will give even
the best roast reason to worry.

SERVES 6

EQUIPMENT: 1 × 20cm deep round
springform cake tin

1 quantity of Savoury Shortcrust Pastry
(see page 206) with 2 teaspoons mixed
seeds added, or use ready-made shortcrust
pastry, defrosted if frozen

A little unsalted butter, for greasing

A little plain flour, for dusting

For the filling

1 butternut squash (about 1.2kg), peeled,
deseeded and cut into 2cm cubes

4 heaped tablespoons dark miso paste

2 tablespoons chunky peanut butter

Juice of 2 limes

1 tablespoon sunflower oil

1 tablespoon toasted sesame oil

1 tablespoon clear honey

2 tablespoons olive oil

1 white onion, finely chopped

3 garlic cloves, finely sliced

2 teaspoons fennel seeds

½ teaspoon dried chilli flakes

250g rainbow chard, stalks and leaves
separated

2 eggs, beaten

Salt and freshly ground black pepper

Continued overleaf >>

1. Unless using ready-made pastry, make the Savoury Shortcrust
Pastry according to the method on page 206, stirring in the
seeds just before you add the egg yolk and water. Wrap in cling
film and leave to rest in the fridge for 30 minutes before using.

2. Meanwhile, preheat the oven to 200°C/180°C fan/Gas Mark 6.
Lightly grease the cake tin with butter.

3. Roll the pastry out on a lightly floured surface into a round
about 3mm thick and line your tin with it, making sure the
edges of the pastry stand a little proud above the rim of the tin.
Trim the edges to even and prick the base all over with a fork,
then chill the pastry case in the fridge for 30 minutes. Don't
be tempted to skip this step, as it helps prevent the pastry
shrinking when baked.

4. Line the pastry case with a piece of non-stick baking paper
and fill it with dried beans, uncooked rice or ceramic baking
beans. Bake the pastry case for 20 minutes. Remove the paper
and baking beans or rice and then bake the pastry case for a
further 10 minutes to ensure that the base is cooked. Remove
from the oven and set aside to cool.

5. To make the filling, arrange the squash cubes in an even
layer in a roasting tin. Mix the miso, peanut butter, lime juice,
sunflower and sesame oils and honey together in a small
mixing bowl and drizzle over the squash. Toss to combine and
season well with salt and pepper. Roast for 25–30 minutes or
until a sharp knife passes through the squash easily and the
edges are starting to catch.

Continued overleaf >>

For the brittle

2 tablespoons sesame oil

2 teaspoons dark soy sauce

1 teaspoon clear honey

40g pumpkin seeds

15g black onion (nigella) seeds

6. Blitz one-quarter of the roasted squash in a food processor until smooth, then scrape into a mixing bowl with the remaining chunky squash.

7. Heat the olive oil in a large frying pan, add the onion and sauté over a medium heat, stirring regularly, for 8–10 minutes until soft and translucent. Stir in the garlic and cook for a minute. Add the fennel seeds and chilli flakes, reduce the heat to low and gently toast the spices for less than a minute.

8. Chop the chard stalks into 1cm pieces, add to the pan and cook for a couple of minutes. Shred the chard leaves and add these too, cooking them until wilted. Mix the chard mixture into the squash and stir the beaten eggs through until thoroughly combined, then spoon the filling into the cooled pastry case.

9. To make the brittle, mix the sesame oil, soy and honey together in a mixing bowl, then stir in the seeds to coat. Drizzle the brittle mixture over the top of the pie and bake for 30 minutes until set.

10. Remove the pie from the oven and leave to cool for 30 minutes before carefully releasing from the tin and slicing into wedges. It will still be lovely and warm.

TIP

YOU CAN PREPARE THE PIE A COUPLE OF DAYS AHEAD: FOLLOW THE RECIPE RIGHT TO THE END, THEN LET THE BAKED PIE COOL COMPLETELY, COVER WITH FOIL AND STORE IN THE FRIDGE. TO SERVE, KEEPING THE FOIL IN PLACE, WARM THROUGH IN AN OVEN PREHEATED TO 190°C/170°C FAN/ GAS MARK 5 FOR 25–30 MINUTES.

VEGEREE

There are so many flavours packed into this veggie take on the classic kedgeree – ginger, curry powder, smoked paprika – that you won't miss the fish. And all you really need on the side is a jar of good-quality mango chutney, or even some feisty lime pickle if you're feeling so inclined. With some freshly squeezed juice and the morning papers, this makes a peerless Sunday brunch.

SERVES 4–6, depending on appetite

25g unsalted butter

2 tablespoons vegetable oil

2 onions, finely chopped

3 garlic cloves, finely chopped

300g brown basmati rice

1 teaspoon ground turmeric

½ teaspoon hot smoked paprika

2 teaspoons medium curry powder

1 teaspoon ground ginger

5 cardamom pods, split open

1 litre vegetable stock

4 eggs

200g French beans, topped (pointy tails left intact)

100g frozen peas

100g baby spinach, washed

1 bunch of chives, finely chopped

50g roasted, salted almonds, roughly chopped

Salt and freshly ground black pepper

To serve

1 lemon, cut into 6 wedges

Mango chutney (optional)

1. Melt the butter with the oil in a large frying pan for which you have a lid (or use foil), stir in the onions and season with salt and pepper. Cover the pan tightly and cook over a low heat for 10 minutes.

2. Add the garlic to the pan and cook for 2 minutes until it smells fragrant but is not browning.

3. Place the rice in a sieve and wash well in several changes of cold water until the water runs clear, then set the sieve over the sink to drain.

4. Meanwhile, add the spices to the pan and cook for a minute until they release their fragrance.

5. Stir in the drained rice and toast it, moving it around the pan with a wooden spoon, for 3 minutes. Pour over the vegetable stock, bring to the boil and cover the pan, then reduce the heat and gently simmer for 25 minutes.

6. Bring a saucepan of water to the boil. Carefully lower in the eggs and set a timer for 6 minutes. Meanwhile, half-fill a mixing bowl with cold water. When the egg cooking time is up, lift the eggs out of the pan and gently tap them on a hard surface to crack the shells. Lower them into the bowl of cold water until you're ready to serve (this makes them easier to shell).

7. Stir the beans, frozen peas and spinach into the rice and cook, uncovered, over a low heat for 10 minutes just to soften the beans.

8. Shell the eggs and cut them into quarters. Arrange over the top of the rice and then remove the pan from the heat.

9. Sprinkle the chives and almonds over the vegeree and serve on warmed plates with a lemon wedge and a spoonful of mango chutney if you like.

THAI GREEN CURRY WITH TOASTED CASHEWS

One thing I've noticed about Thai cooking is that the sauce always takes centre stage – and rightly so. My green curry, which uses soft soaked cashew nuts almost like a vegetable, is extremely simple to make, not that your guests will ever guess. What's more, it happens to be vegan.

SERVES 4

200g raw cashew nuts

2 tablespoons coconut oil or vegetable oil

1 small bunch of spring onions, white and green parts finely sliced

1 thumb of fresh root ginger, peeled and grated

1 bunch of coriander, stalks and leaves separated, stalks finely sliced and leaves reserved for scattering over the curry

3 garlic cloves, finely sliced

2 lemon grass sticks, very finely shredded

2 green chillies, finely chopped

2 × 400ml cans coconut milk

200g curly kale or spinach, washed and tough stalks removed

200g mangetout, halved lengthways

Juice of 1 lime

Salt and freshly ground black pepper

Cooked rice, to serve

1. Put half the cashews in a bowl, pour over warm water to cover and add a pinch of salt. Leave to soak for 30 minutes.

2. Meanwhile, heat a dry frying pan over a medium heat, add the remaining cashews and toast until golden. Transfer the cashews to a bowl to cool.

3. Heat the oil in a medium saucepan, add the spring onions, ginger, coriander stalks, garlic, lemon grass and chillies with a pinch of salt and sauté over a low heat, stirring regularly, for 10 minutes until soft.

4. Drain the soaked cashews, add to the pan with the coconut milk and gently simmer for 20–25 minutes. Stir through the vegetables and cook for a further 5 minutes or until the greens have wilted; the mangetout will soften in the residual heat. Remove the pan from the heat, squeeze in the lime juice and season to taste with salt and pepper.

5. Scatter over the toasted cashews and coriander leaves and serve with rice.

SUGAR SNAP PAELLA WITH GREMOLATA

Spanish cooks can get a bit purist about paella, and doubtless this meat- and seafood-free version would raise an eyebrow or two among the aficionados of Valencia. Well, perhaps we'll just keep it to ourselves then. A big pan of this in the middle of the table, everyone cheerfully digging in…just the idea is enough to get me in a party mood.

SERVES 4

EQUIPMENT: 1 × 28cm frying pan, 4–6cm deep; a griddle pan or heavy-based frying pan

3 tablespoons olive oil

3 white onions, finely sliced

3 garlic cloves, finely sliced

3 large tomatoes on the vine, roughly chopped

2 roasted red peppers from a jar, drained and roughly chopped

1 teaspoon hot smoked paprika

Large pinch of saffron threads

800ml hot vegetable stock

200g paella rice

2 corn on the cob (about 100g each)

150g sugar snap peas, finely sliced

Salt and freshly ground black pepper

To serve (optional)

Gremolata (see page 215)

1 lemon, cut into 6 wedges

1. Heat the olive oil in the 28cm frying pan over a medium heat. Add the onions with a pinch of salt, cover the pan with a lid and cook, stirring occasionally, for 5 minutes until they are soft and translucent. Stir in the garlic and cook for a couple of minutes.

2. Add the tomatoes, peppers and paprika to the pan and cook, stirring, for a few minutes until the tomatoes start to soften. Meanwhile, add the saffron threads to the hot vegetable stock and leave to soak for a couple of minutes.

3. Pour the saffron-infused stock into the pan, then scatter over the rice and bring to the boil. Reduce the heat to a low setting and leave to cook, without stirring, for 20 minutes until all the stock has been absorbed.

4. While the rice is cooking, heat the griddle pan or heavy-based frying pan over a high heat for 5 minutes. Add the corn cobs and char all over until they are blackened in places. This usually takes 8–12 minutes, depending on the level of sugars in the corn.

5. Remove the cobs from the pan and leave to cool slightly, then stand upright on a chopping board and use a sharp knife to slice down each cob all the way around to remove the kernels.

6. Scatter the sugar snaps and charred corn over the top of the paella and let them cook in the steam from the pan for 4 minutes. Then remove the pan from the heat and leave the paella to rest for 10 minutes before serving.

7. Season the paella to taste with black pepper and serve with the Gremolata spooned over the top and the lemon wedges on the side, if you like.

TIP

RESIST THE TEMPTATION TO STIR THE RICE WHILE IT COOKS BECAUSE LEAVING IT UNDISTURBED ENCOURAGES A FLAVOURSOME, CRUNCHY CRUST TO FORM ON THE BASE OF THE PAN, AS DOES LEAVING THE COOKED PAELLA TO REST BEFORE SERVING.

CRANBERRY & PORCINI NUT ROAST

Nut roasts get a bit of a bad press, but this may just be the recipe to change all that. Yes, it requires some effort (in fact, it might be my longest-ever recipe), but with its intensely flavoured porcini mushrooms, sweet butternut squash and zippy cranberries, it's a sound investment, I promise you. On Christmas Day, with all the trimmings, it will give roast turkey a good run for its money.

SERVES 8

EQUIPMENT: 1 × 900g loaf tin

400g can chickpeas

1 teaspoon hot smoked paprika

1 teaspoon dried oregano

½ butternut squash (about 400g), peeled, deseeded and cut into 2cm pieces

6 garlic cloves, unpeeled

½ small bunch of sage, leaves picked

6 tablespoons olive oil

30g dried porcini mushrooms

400ml warm water

3 shallots, finely chopped

2 celery sticks, finely chopped

125g risotto rice

125ml dry white wine

A few sprigs of thyme, leaves picked

150g hazelnuts, roughly chopped

1 red chilli, finely chopped

Juice of 1 lemon, or more to taste

40g breadcrumbs (any type), toasted

300g frozen cranberries

4 tablespoons caster sugar

Salt and freshly ground black pepper

Continued overleaf >>

1. Preheat the oven to 200°C/180°C fan/Gas Mark 6.

2. Drain the can of chickpeas over a bowl to catch the liquid, which you'll use later. Dry the chickpeas well on kitchen paper, then roughly chop them. Toss the chickpeas, paprika, oregano, squash, garlic cloves and sage leaves in a shallow roasting tin with 4 tablespoons of the olive oil and a generous pinch of salt and pepper. Roast for 35 minutes, turning every 10 minutes, until the garlic cloves are beginning to caramelize. Remove from the oven and leave until cool enough to handle, then squeeze the garlic cloves out of their skins and mash them with the squash and chickpeas using a fork until you have a chunky consistency. Set aside.

3. While the squash and chickpea mixture finishes roasting and cooling, cover the dried porcini with the measured warm water in a bowl and leave to soak for 15 minutes.

4. Heat the remaining 2 tablespoons of olive oil in a heavy-based saucepan, add the shallots and celery and cook over a medium heat, stirring regularly, for 10 minutes until they are soft. Add the rice and stir well to evenly distribute, then pour in the white wine and cook, stirring continuously, until it has been completely absorbed.

5. Strain the soaked porcini through a fine sieve over a bowl to catch the soaking liquid. Add the porcini to the pan with the thyme. Then add the porcini soaking liquid a ladleful at a time, stirring regularly until each addition has been absorbed before adding the next.

Continued overleaf >>

To serve (optional)

Onion Gravy (see page 216)

Lemony Roasties with Crispy Kale (see page 127)

Caramelized Fennel with Pangrattato (see page 126)

6. When all the stock has been absorbed and the rice is cooked (it should be soft throughout, but still have a visible white speck in the middle), tip the mixture into a large mixing bowl and combine it with the chickpea and squash mixture. Add the hazelnuts, chilli, lemon juice and breadcrumbs, stir really well and taste, seasoning with a little more salt or lemon juice if you like. When you're happy with the flavour, stir through the reserved chickpea water to bind the mixture.

7. Reduce the oven temperature to 180°C/160°C fan/Gas Mark 4.

8. Place the cranberries in a small saucepan with the sugar and cook over a low heat until just softened. Drain away half the juice.

9. Line the base and sides of the loaf tin with non-stick baking paper. Spread half the cranberry mixture over the base with a spatula. Add half the veggie mixture and pack down with the spatula. Spread the remaining cranberries over the top, then layer with the remaining veggie mixture, packing it down firmly with the spatula to smooth the surface.

10. Bake the nut roast on the middle shelf of the oven for an hour. The exposed top will become crispy and browned.

11. Remove the nut roast from the oven and leave to cool in the tin for at least 30 minutes. Then invert onto a serving platter and give the base of the tin a sharp whack. Lift away the baking paper to reveal the sticky cranberry top. Serve with the various accompaniments, of your choosing.

TIPS

YOU CAN PREPARE THE DISH TO THE END OF STEP 8 A FEW DAYS BEFORE CHRISTMAS, COOL, COVER AND REFRIGERATE, THEN ASSEMBLE AND BAKE THE NUT ROAST ON CHRISTMAS MORNING. THE MIXTURE ALSO MAKES A LOVELY STUFFING.

MELT-IN-THE-MIDDLE POTATO CAKES WITH QUICK PICKLES

This dish has 'Mother's Day brunch' written all over it. Coax the kids into giving a helping hand the day before – they will love shaping the mixture into little patties – and then in the morning it will just be a matter of sautéing them and combining the ingredients for the quick pickles. Dads looking for brownie points take heed.

MAKES ABOUT 10 potato cakes

For the quick pickles

1 cucumber, halved lengthways and seeds scraped out with the tip of a teaspoon

1 red onion, finely sliced

Juice of ½ lemon

2 tablespoons apple cider vinegar

2 teaspoons caster sugar

2 teaspoons salt

1 teaspoon dried dill

For the potato cakes

4–5 potatoes (about 750g), peeled and cut into 3cm chunks

100g frozen peas

100g spinach, washed

2 tablespoons crème fraîche

1 tablespoon wholegrain mustard

125–150g ball of mozzarella cheese or, if you can find them, mozzarella pearls

1 egg

50g panko breadcrumbs (see page 120)

Vegetable oil, for frying

Salt and freshly ground black pepper

1. First, make the quick pickles. Cut the cucumber halves into 2mm-thick slices and toss with the onion and other pickling ingredients in a non-metallic bowl. Then use your hands to scrunch the vegetables and work in the sugar, salt and dill. Place a saucer over the top of the veg and weigh down with a food can or jar, then set aside while you make the potato cakes.

2. Bring a large saucepan of water to the boil, lower in the potatoes and cook for 10–12 minutes until completely soft to the point of a knife. Remove with a slotted spoon to a colander and leave to cool and let as much steam evaporate as possible.

3. Add the peas to the potato cooking water and boil for 1 minute or until they rise to the surface, then drain and place in a mixing bowl.

4. Place the spinach in a large saucepan with just the water left clinging to the leaves after washing. Cover the pan with a lid and cook over a medium heat for 1 minute until just wilted. Transfer the spinach to a sieve over the sink and press with the back of a wooden spoon to out squeeze out as much water as you can.

5. Add the potatoes to the bowl with the peas and use a potato masher to mash the potatoes until smooth. Squeeze out any remaining water from the spinach with your hands, then chop it roughly before adding to the mash along with the crème fraîche and mustard. Taste and add more salt, pepper and/or mustard depending on your preference.

Continued overleaf >>

6. Take a handful of the potato mixture and flatten it with your palm. Place a cherry tomato-sized piece of mozzarella, or a mozzarella pearl, in the centre of the potato mixture, fold the sides of the mixture over the cheese and then flatten the mixture around the mozzarella so that it's entirely encased in the middle and you have a patty shape. Place on a tray lined with non-stick baking paper. Repeat with the remaining potato mixture and mozzarella – you should have about 10 cakes. Place the tray in the fridge for 20 minutes to cool and firm up the patties, which will help them to hold their shape when you fry them.

7. Beat the egg in a wide bowl and place the breadcrumbs on a plate. Dip each potato cake first in the egg and then in the breadcrumbs, coating both sides.

8. Heat enough vegetable oil to coat the base of a large frying pan over a medium heat and cook the potato cakes, in batches to avoid overcrowding the pan, for 4–5 minutes on each side until crisp and golden. Place the cooked cakes on a baking sheet and keep warm in a low oven while you cook the remainder.

9. To serve, place a spoonful of the pickles alongside each potato cake (2 cakes per person is about right) and then break into them to reveal the melting middle.

PUMPKIN, WALNUT & SAGE CROSTATA

A crostata is an Italian baked tart, often with a wonderfully rustic free-form pastry case. With its sweet pumpkin filling and tangy Stilton topping, this dramatic veggie centrepiece is the essence of Christmas.

SERVES 6

1 quantity of Walnutty Pastry (see page 209)

A little plain flour, for dusting

For the filling

1 pumpkin (about 750g), peeled, deseeded and cut into 2cm-thick wedges

4 shallots, quartered

4 garlic cloves, peeled and left whole

½ bunch of sage, leaves picked

Olive oil, for drizzling

50g walnuts

1 teaspoon clear honey

2 teaspoons wholegrain mustard

2 tablespoons apple cider vinegar

Pinch of dried chilli flakes

30g unsalted butter

12 sage leaves

40g blue cheese, such as Stilton, crumbled

Salt and freshly ground black pepper

1. First, start making the filling. Preheat the oven to 200°C/180°C fan/Gas Mark 6.

2. Divide the pumpkin wedges between 2 large shallow roasting tins with the shallots, garlic and sage. Drizzle over enough olive oil to coat and season well with salt and pepper. Roast for 25 minutes.

3. Meanwhile, make the Walnutty Pastry according to the method on page 209, then wrap in cling film and leave to rest in the fridge for 30 minutes.

4. Remove both tins from the oven and set one tin of roast pumpkin aside for later. Add the walnuts to the other tin of pumpkin and roast for a further 10 minutes. Remove from the oven, keeping the oven on, and scrape the walnut and pumpkin mixture into a food processor. Add the honey, mustard, vinegar and chilli flakes and blitz on a high speed. While the processor is running, drizzle in enough olive oil, about 4 tablespoons, to turn the consistency of the mixture from chunky to smooth. Check the seasoning and adjust with salt and pepper to taste.

5. Line a large baking sheet with non-stick baking paper. Roll the pastry out on a lightly floured surface to a rough 25cm circle, about 3mm thick – the dough will still be quite crumbly because of the walnuts, but all the more delicious for it. Transfer the pastry circle to the lined baking sheet. Spoon the filling mixture into the centre of the pastry, leaving a border of about 4cm around the edge. Arrange the reserved pumpkin wedges on top of the filling. Lift the pastry border up around the edge of the vegetables and crimp. Don't worry if the pastry breaks – just patch together any gaps. Bake for 30 minutes.

6. While the crostata is baking, line a plate with kitchen paper. Melt the butter in a frying pan, and when it starts to foam, scatter the sage leaves evenly around the pan so that none overlap. Use a spatula to turn the leaves over and crisp them up – this should take no longer than 45 seconds. Transfer the sage leaves to the lined plate to crisp up further.

7. Remove the crostata from the oven and sprinkle over the blue cheese and crispy sage leaves. Leave to cool and for the blue cheese to melt into the crostata for 15 minutes before slicing.

TUSCAN PARCELS

Once you've made the ratatouille, this is little more than an assembly job. Shop-bought puff pastry works a dream here, but make sure you use the all-butter variety. If the black olive/ pine nut combo doesn't light your fire, a touch of feta and a sprinkle of pumpkin seeds offers an excellent alternative. This makes a great Sunday brunch dish along with some fried eggs, to which you can add some chorizo for any ardent meat-eaters present.

MAKES 8

½ quantity of Oven-roasted Ratatouille (see page 31)

500g ready-to-roll all-butter puff pastry, defrosted if frozen

A little plain flour, for dusting

1 beaten egg, to glaze

50g pitted black olives

25g pine nuts

1 small bunch of oregano, leaves picked, plus extra to garnish

Salt and freshly ground black pepper

Whipped ricotta cheese or crème fraîche, to serve

1. Make the Oven-roasted Ratatouille according to the method on page 31, then leave to cool completely.

2. Line a baking sheet with non-stick baking paper. Roll the puff pastry out on a lightly floured surface into a large rectangle measuring about 40 × 28cm, trimming it so that the sides are straight. Cut the rectangle lengthways in half, then across into thirds to make 6 equal (about 13cm) squares. Place the pastry squares on the lined baking sheet and brush with beaten egg.

3. Spoon 2 generous tablespoons of ratatouille into the centre of each pastry square, leaving about 2cm around all four sides. Sprinkle the olives, pine nuts and oregano over the ratatouille and season with salt and pepper. Pull the corners of the square to the middle, leaving a 1cm gap in the centre so that the filling is visible. Brush the exposed pastry with the beaten egg and sprinkle with pepper.

4. Preheat the oven to 200°C/180°C fan/Gas Mark 6. Meanwhile, chill the parcels in the freezer for 10 minutes.

5. Bake the parcels for 15–18 minutes until puffed up and golden. Serve hot from the oven, or transfer to a wire rack to cool if not serving straight away. Garnish with extra oregano and serve with a spoonful of whipped ricotta or crème fraîche.

TIP

YOU CAN MAKE THE RATATOUILLE UP TO 3 DAYS IN ADVANCE, COVERING AND STORING IT IN THE FRIDGE ONCE COMPLETELY COOLED.

ROASTED POTATO, BEETROOT & RHUBARB CRUMBLE

I'll be the first to admit that rhubarb and beetroot are unlikely bedfellows. But trust me, the combo of earthy sweetness and zippy tartness works surprisingly well. Top tip: cooking the crumble separately keeps it nice and crispy while making sure that any leftovers the next day will be every bit as delicious. This is great served with vegetarian sausages and wilted greens.

SERVES 4–6

EQUIPMENT: 1 × 20cm square roasting tin

750g Charlotte or other small waxy potatoes

3 tablespoons vegetable oil

1 red onion, thinly sliced

1 sprig of rosemary

150ml soured cream

100ml double cream

200ml vegetable stock

3 bay leaves

3 cooked, peeled beetroot (about 300g), cut into 2cm pieces

200g rhubarb, trimmed and sliced into 5mm pieces

Salt and freshly ground black pepper

For the crumble topping

100g plain flour

100g rolled porridge oats

100g unsalted butter, cut into 1cm cubes

50g mixed seeds (I like linseeds, sunflower seeds and poppy seeds)

A few sprigs of thyme, leaves picked

Salt and freshly ground black pepper

1. Preheat the oven to 200°C/180°C fan/Gas Mark 6.

2. Bring a large saucepan of water to the boil. Gently lower the potatoes into the pan and boil them for 12 minutes or until a sharp knife passes through them easily. Drain the potatoes, and when they're cool enough to handle, halve any larger ones with a sharp knife so that they're all roughly the size of a golf ball or smaller.

3. Warm the oil in the roasting tin in the oven for a few minutes. Remove from the oven and toss the boiled potatoes in the oil along with the onion and rosemary. Season with salt and pepper and roast for 20 minutes until the potatoes are golden and crisp in places.

4. While the potatoes are roasting, pour both creams and the vegetable stock into a small saucepan, add the bay leaves and bring to the boil. Remove the pan from the heat and set aside to infuse for 30 minutes.

5. Make the crumble topping by placing all the ingredients in a mixing bowl and rubbing together with your fingertips until the mixture resembles coarse breadcrumbs.

6. Remove the potatoes from the oven, add the beetroot and rhubarb to the tin and stir to combine. Lift the bay leaves from the infused cream and discard, then pour the cream over the vegetables in the tin. Bake for 35 minutes until bright pink, bubbling and catching at the sides.

7. About halfway through the beetroot and rhubarb baking time, spread the crumble topping mixture in an even layer in a large shallow roasting tin and bake on a separate shelf of the oven for 15 minutes until golden and crisp.

8. Serve the crumble topping on the side for everyone to sprinkle over the creamy vegetables.

BOURGUIGNONNE PIE WITH MASH

A bowl of super-buttery root veg mash, topped with a rich, autumnal stew made with mushrooms, red wine and my beloved puy lentils: what could be more vivifying? Oh, and if you've not yet sampled crispy capers (I'm a recent convert), get ready for a revelation.

SERVES 4–6

For the mash

1 swede, peeled and cut into 3cm chunks

2 parsnips, peeled and cut into 3cm chunks

500g floury potatoes, peeled and cut into 3cm chunks

25g unsalted butter

⅛ whole nutmeg, grated

A splash of milk

Salt and freshly ground black pepper

For the bourguignonne

2 tablespoons olive oil, plus an extra splash

2 white onions, finely sliced

1 large carrot, peeled and finely diced

3 garlic cloves, finely sliced

400g raw beetroot, peeled and cut into 3cm pieces

3 bay leaves

½ small bunch of thyme

2 tablespoons tomato purée

200ml red wine

500ml vegetable stock

4 shallots, quartered

150g chestnut mushrooms, quartered

250g pouch ready-cooked puy lentils

Salt and freshly ground black pepper

For the crispy capers

4 tablespoons olive oil

3 tablespoons capers, drained and dried

1 small bunch of flat leaf parsley, leaves picked and chopped

1. First, make the mash. Place the swede and parsnips in a large saucepan and cover with cold water. Set over a high heat, cover the pan and bring to the boil. After the veg has been boiling fast for 5 minutes, add the potatoes, bring back to the boil and boil for a further 10–15 minutes until a sharp knife passes through each vegetable easily. Drain in a colander and return everything to the pan. Cover the pan again and shake well to fluff the vegetables up. Add the butter, nutmeg and milk, then use a potato masher to mash the vegetables until smooth. Taste and season with salt and pepper. Set aside and keep warm.

2. Now turn your attention to the bourguignonne. Heat the olive oil in a large saucepan over a medium heat and stir in the onions and carrot with a pinch of salt. Cook, stirring regularly, for 10 minutes until the vegetables are soft. Add the garlic, beetroot, bay leaves and thyme and cook for a further 5 minutes. Stir in the tomato purée, wine and stock and bring up to the boil, then reduce the heat and simmer for 20 minutes.

3. Meanwhile, warm the splash of olive oil in a large frying pan over a high heat and add the shallots and mushrooms with a pinch of salt. Turn the heat down to medium and cook, stirring regularly, for 10–12 minutes until brown. Add the shallots and mushrooms to the bourguignonne along with the lentils and simmer for a further 10 minutes. Taste and adjust the seasoning with salt and pepper before removing the bay leaves.

4. Wipe the frying pan out with kitchen paper and heat the olive oil for the capers over a high heat until it's shimmering. Add the capers to the hot oil and cook until they open like blooming buds – this should take about 30 seconds if the oil is hot enough, but if not, be patient, as the oil just needs to come up to temperature. Remove with a slotted spoon to a plate lined with kitchen paper.

5. Divide the mash between warmed plates and spoon the bourguignonne over the top. Scatter the crispy capers and chopped parsley over each serving.

BEET WELLINGTON

This is as dramatic a dish as any beef Wellington. On New Year's Eve, carved at the table to reveal the striking crimson-coloured beets within, it makes for a truly memorable meal and the meaty mushrooms, rich red wine and zingy goats' cheese really punch up the umami flavours.

SERVES 8

4 raw, unpeeled beetroot, all roughly the same size and shape, scrubbed and halved around the middle

1 tablespoon balsamic or red wine vinegar

Olive oil, for drizzling and oiling

2 × 320g sheets of ready-rolled all-butter puff pastry, defrosted if frozen

A little plain flour, for dusting

100g unsalted butter

4 shallots, finely chopped

3 garlic cloves, finely sliced

250g chestnut mushrooms, diced into 5mm pieces

175ml full-bodied red wine

200g spinach, washed and dried

150g soft goats' cheese

1 beaten egg, to glaze

1 teaspoon black onion (nigella) seeds (optional)

Salt and freshly ground black pepper

Onion Gravy (see page 216), to serve

1. Preheat the oven to 200°C/180°C fan/Gas Mark 6. Toss the halved beetroot in a shallow roasting tin with the vinegar and a drizzle of olive oil. Season well with salt and pepper and cover the tin tightly with foil. Roast on the middle shelf of the oven for 1 hour or until a sharp knife passes through the beetroot easily. Remove from the oven, lift away the foil and set aside.

2. Unroll a sheet of puff pastry on a lightly floured surface. Trim the pastry to a rectangle measuring 30cm × 15cm × 3mm. Place the pastry on a lightly oiled baking sheet and top with a second baking sheet, also lightly oiled. Bake for 20 minutes, then remove from the oven and set aside, keeping the oven on.

3. Melt the butter in a large frying pan and sauté the shallots over a medium heat for 6 minutes until soft. Stir in the garlic and cook for a couple of minutes. Remove one-third of the shallot mixture to a bowl and reserve. Stir the mushrooms into the remaining shallot mixture in the pan and season with salt and pepper. Cook for 8 minutes until the mushrooms are golden and have released all their liquid and it has evaporated. Pour in the red wine, turn the heat up to high and cook until it has all been absorbed. Lift the mushrooms onto a plate with a slotted spoon to drain off some of the butter.

4. Add the spinach to the pan and cook over a medium heat until wilted. Scrape the spinach into a sieve and leave until cool enough to handle, then squeeze out as much water as you can. Transfer to the bowl with the reserved shallot mixture and stir to combine, then crumble in the goats' cheese and stir again.

5. To assemble, arrange the spinach and goats' cheese down the centre of the baked pastry sheet, leaving a 3cm border either side of the mixture. Place the beetroot on top of the spinach (you may not need all the beetroot, depending on their size). Pile the mushrooms on top of the beetroot. You will have quite a mound now!

6. Unroll the second pastry sheet and make sure it measures about 35 × 20cm, rolling it out on a lightly floured surface as necessary. Drape it over the filling, tucking the edges underneath the cooked pastry base. Brush with beaten egg to glaze and chill in the freezer for 20 minutes. Brush with beaten egg again and decorate with pastry shapes (brush these with beaten egg too) or with a sprinkling of black onion seeds. Bake for 45–50 minutes until golden brown and flaky. Serve hot with the Onion Gravy.

VEG ON THE SIDE

I often feel sorry for side dishes – always the bridesmaid and all that. However, with a clever twist here and an unexpected ingredient there, a humble veggie side can be transformed into something truly magnificent.

PARSNIP POLENTA CHIPS WITH PEPPERCORN SAUCE

Don't be deterred by the slightly fiddly process involved in this recipe. These cheesy parsnip chips are beyond moreish and well worth the effort. Serve them with the Salt-baked Celeriac with Apple, Kale & Blue Cheese on page 134.

SERVES 4–6 as a side

For the parsnip chips

600g parsnips, peeled and cut into 1cm-wide, 3cm-long sticks

100g polenta

50g Parmesan cheese, finely grated

50g plain flour

2 eggs

100ml vegetable or sunflower oil

Salt and freshly ground black pepper

For the peppercorn sauce

50g unsalted butter

1 large or 2 small shallots, finely chopped

1–2 teaspoons black peppercorns, lightly crushed

2 tablespoons green peppercorns, lightly crushed

100ml brandy

1 tablespoon dark miso paste

100ml hot water

75ml double cream

Salt and freshly ground black pepper

1. Preheat the oven to 220°C/200°C fan/Gas Mark 7.

2. Bring a large saucepan of water to the boil. Lower the parsnip sticks into the water and boil for 5 minutes until a sharp knife passes through them easily.

3. Drain the parsnip sticks in a colander and leave them to sit, letting the steam escape and the sticks cool slightly for a few minutes.

4. Meanwhile, mix the polenta and Parmesan together in a large mixing bowl. Place the flour on a plate and season well with salt and pepper, then beat the eggs in a wide bowl.

5. Toss the parsnip sticks in the seasoned flour, then dip into the beaten egg and finally toss in the polenta to coat.

6. Pour the oil into a large shallow roasting tin and heat in the oven for 4 minutes. Remove from the oven, add the coated parsnip sticks to the hot oil, taking care as the oil may sizzle and spit, and use a spatula to turn and coat them. Roast for 20–25 minutes, turning twice during this time, until crisp and golden all over.

7. While the parsnip chips are roasting, make the peppercorn sauce. Melt the butter in a saucepan, add the shallots and stir to coat, then sauté over a medium heat for 5 minutes until soft and translucent. Add the peppercorns and cook for a couple of minutes to toast them slightly. Then pour in the brandy and cook until reduced by half. Stir in the miso paste and measured hot water and cook at a steady simmer for 5 minutes. Finally, turn the heat down to low and stir in the cream. Cook until the mixture is slightly thickened, but don't let the mixture boil – a steady simmer is fine. Taste and adjust the seasoning with salt and pepper.

8. Remove the parsnip chips from the oven and transfer to a plate lined with kitchen paper to absorb the excess oil. Serve hot with the warm peppercorn sauce for dipping.

CELERIAC & CHEDDAR CRUMBLE

After a brisk walk on a winter's day, this more than just about anything is what I crave. Comfort food doesn't get any comfier.

SERVES 4 as a light main or as a side

EQUIPMENT: 1 × 20cm square ovenproof dish or roasting tin

3 tablespoons olive oil

2 red onions, roughly sliced

1 celeriac (about 700g), roughly peeled and cut into 2cm cubes

1 large sweet potato (about 400g), peeled and cut into 2cm cubes

3 garlic cloves, finely chopped

4 sprigs of rosemary, leaves picked and chopped

100ml water

200ml crème fraîche

2 teaspoons wholegrain mustard

Grated zest and juice of 1 unwaxed lemon

125g Cheddar cheese, grated

100g plain flour

50g unsalted butter, cut into 1cm cubes, plus a little extra for greasing

25g flaked almonds

Salt and freshly ground black pepper

1. Preheat the oven to 200°C/180°C fan/Gas Mark 6.

2. Heat the olive oil in a large frying pan over a medium heat, add the onions and sauté for 6–7 minutes until starting to soften. Add the celeriac and sweet potato and cook, stirring regularly, for 5–7 minutes until just starting to colour, then add the garlic and rosemary and cook for a further 2 minutes. Pour in the measured water and cook, without stirring, for about 10 minutes until the vegetables have softened and all the water has evaporated, otherwise the crumble filling will turn soggy.

3. Lightly grease the ovenproof dish or roasting tin with butter. Mix the crème fraîche, mustard, lemon zest and juice and 100g of the Cheddar together in a large mixing bowl. Season well with salt and pepper, then stir in the vegetable mixture to coat. Tip the creamy vegetables into the greased dish or tin.

4. Place the flour in a mixing bowl, add the butter and the remaining Cheddar and rub in with your fingertips until the mixture becomes a rubble of crumble, then mix in the almonds. Season the crumble with salt and pepper and sprinkle on top of the vegetable mixture.

5. Bake on the middle shelf of the oven for 30–35 minutes until the crumble topping is golden and crisp. Serve hot.

TIP

THE CRUMBLE CAN BE STORED IN THE FREEZER FOR UP TO 2 MONTHS. SIMPLY ASSEMBLE UP TO THE END OF STEP 4, THEN COVER TIGHTLY WITH CLING FILM AND FREEZE. DEFROST THE CRUMBLE THOROUGHLY BEFORE BAKING AS ABOVE.

MAPLE-GLAZED PARSNIP MASH WITH CAVOLO NERO & POMEGRANATE

This recipe and the one opposite both use exactly the same ingredients, but the resulting flavours and textures are wildly different. This dish has softer textures than the salad, with the beans being stewed and lightly mashed as opposed to quickly roasted, and the kale gently wilted instead of crisped up in the oven. An extremely comforting dish for an autumnal evening.

SERVES 4 as a generous starter or side

EQUIPMENT: 1 × 28cm ovenproof non-stick frying pan

5 tablespoons olive oil

2 garlic cloves, finely sliced

600g jar cannellini beans

1kg parsnips (750g prepared weight), cut into ribbons with a Y-shaped vegetable peeler

2 tablespoons maple syrup

Juice of 1 lemon

200g cavolo nero, well washed

2 tablespoons water

½ × 125g pack pomegranate seeds

Salt and freshly ground black pepper

1. Heat 2 tablespoons of the olive oil in a saucepan over a medium–low heat, add the garlic and sauté for a couple of minutes. Pour in the beans with their liquid from the jar and simmer for 12 minutes.

2. While the beans are cooking, toss the parsnip ribbons with the maple syrup, half the lemon juice and 2 tablespoons of olive oil in a mixing bowl. Season with salt and pepper.

3. Strip the leaves from the cavolo nero stalks by grasping each leaf at the base in the centre and pulling firmly towards the tip.

4. When the beans are cooked, use a potato masher to mash about half of them in the pan until slightly creamy. Add the remaining lemon juice, then season to taste with salt and pepper.

5. Heat the frying pan over a medium heat, add the parsnip ribbons and cook, turning them regularly with tongs, for 7–9 minutes until golden and sticky in places. Remove from the pan and keep warm in a low oven.

6. Wipe out the pan with a piece of kitchen paper. Add the remaining olive oil along with the measured water and cook the cavolo nero over a medium heat for 2–3 minutes until wilted.

7. Spoon the creamy beans onto a warmed plate and arrange the cavolo nero and parsnips on top. Scatter over the pomegranate seeds and serve immediately.

TIP

I'VE SPECIFIED JARRED BEANS IN BOTH THESE RECIPES BECAUSE THEY'RE COOKED IN SMALLER BATCHES THAN CANNED BEANS AND THEREFORE WITH MORE CARE, AND ARE BOTTLED IN A REALLY FLAVOURFUL STOCK, WHICH WILL ADD TO THE FINAL FLAVOUR OF YOUR DISH.

MAPLE-GLAZED PARSNIP, CAVOLO NERO & POMEGRANATE SALAD

This very different variation on the same ingredients is, for me, the ultimate winter salad. It works well served with a generous wedge of your favourite veggie pie.

SERVES 4 as a generous starter or side

65ml olive oil, plus extra for drizzling if needed

2 tablespoons maple syrup

2 garlic cloves, unpeeled

1kg parsnips, peeled, halved lengthways and cut into irregular-shaped 2cm pieces (about 750g prepared weight)

600g jar cannellini beans, drained

200g cavolo nero, well washed and dried, torn from the stalks (see opposite)

Zest and juice of 1 unwaxed lemon

½ × 125g pack pomegranate seeds

Salt and freshly ground black pepper

Salsa Verde (see page 215), to serve

1. Preheat the oven to 200°C/180°C fan/Gas Mark 6.

2. Measure 50ml of the olive oil into a large shallow roasting tin and add the maple syrup and garlic cloves. Then add the parsnips and toss around to coat in the oil and syrup before seasoning with salt and pepper. Roast on the middle shelf of the oven for 20 minutes.

3. While the parsnips are roasting, spread the beans out on a plate between 2 pieces of kitchen paper to dry out.

4. After the parsnips have been roasting for 20 minutes, remove from the oven and push them to one side of the tin. Spread the beans over the other half of the tin in an even layer. If, however, the ingredients are looking too crowded, simply put the beans in a separate roasting tin and drizzle with olive oil. Roast for 15 minutes.

5. Meanwhile, tear the cavolo nero leaves into large pieces in another shallow roasting tin (they will shrink as they cook) and then use your hands to massage the remaining 15ml (tablespoon) of olive oil and some salt into them. Roast the cavolo nero for the final 5 minutes of the parsnip and bean roasting time.

6. Remove the parsnips and beans from the oven, turn the oven off and leave the cavolo nero inside while it's cooling down to let the leaves dry out and crisp up. This should take about 15 minutes.

7. When cool enough to handle, squeeze the garlic from its skins and mix through the warm parsnips with the lemon juice. Arrange the parsnips, beans and crispy cavolo nero on a large platter, topping with the pomegranate seeds, lemon zest and a good helping of Salsa Verde.

PARSNIP RÖSTI WITH SPICY SALSA

This recipe is for one big rösti, which can be ceremoniously divvied up at the table. But if you'd rather make smaller, individual ones, do feel free. The quantities for my spicy salsa are more guide than gospel, as are the ingredients themselves. If you're not keen on coriander, for example, and you're addicted to avocado, swap away.

SERVES 4 as a starter or side

EQUIPMENT: 1 × 25cm ovenproof non-stick frying pan

For the rösti

300g parsnips, peeled and grated

1 potato, peeled and grated

1 teaspoon salt

1 egg, beaten

2 tablespoons plain flour

2 teaspoons black onion (nigella) seeds

3 tablespoons vegetable oil

For the spicy salsa

1 shallot, finely chopped

3 tomatoes, roughly chopped

1 red chilli, deseeded and finely chopped

1 garlic clove, finely chopped

2 teaspoons red wine vinegar

3 tablespoons extra virgin olive oil

½ small bunch of coriander, leaves picked and chopped

Salt and freshly ground black pepper

To serve (optional)

1 tablespoon vegetable oil

1 tablespoon capers in brine, drained and dried on kitchen paper

1. For the rösti, toss the parsnips and potato with the salt in a large mixing bowl. Set aside for 20 minutes for the salt to draw out the excess moisture from the vegetables.

2. Preheat the oven to 200°C/180°C fan/Gas Mark 6.

3. Meanwhile, make the salsa. Mix all the ingredients except the coriander together in a bowl, season generously and set aside.

4. Lay a clean tea towel in a colander and scrape the parsnip and potato mixture into the centre of the cloth. Gather up the sides and squeeze to extract as much liquid as you can. Turn the parsnip and potato mixture into a large mixing bowl and stir in the egg, flour and black onion seeds. Mix well until no patches of flour are visible.

5. Heat the vegetable oil in the ovenproof frying pan and use a wooden spoon to spread the rösti mixture across the base of the pan and flatten the top. Cook over a low–medium heat for 10 minutes until you can lift the base with a spatula and it looks golden in colour.

6. Use 2 spatulas to flip the rösti. Alternatively, place a flat plate over the top of the pan and hold it in place as you invert the pan and plate together so that the rösti falls onto the plate, then slip the rösti back into the pan so that the crisp, golden base is now facing upwards. Transfer the pan to the oven for 12–15 minutes until the rösti is thoroughly cooked through.

7. While the rösti finishes cooking, if making the crispy capers to serve, heat the vegetable oil in a small frying pan over a high heat. Add the capers to the hot oil and cook until they open like blooming buds – this should take about 30 seconds if the oil is hot enough. Remove with a slotted spoon to a plate lined with kitchen paper.

8. Remove the rösti from the oven and leave to cool for 5 minutes before inverting onto on a board or flat plate and slicing into 4 wedges. Stir the chopped coriander leaves into the salsa and spoon a little salsa over the top of each slice. If you've prepared them, scatter the crispy capers over the top too.

CARROT, GINGER & PEANUT SLAW

If I'm cooking something particularly hearty and rich, I'll make sure to serve something light and refreshing on the side. This slaw is one of my go-to recipes, and it works especially well with a wedge of the Miso Squash & Chard Pie on page 81.

SERVES 4 as a side

For the dressing

2 tablespoons toasted sesame oil

Juice of 2 limes

1½ tablespoons soy sauce

1 teaspoon clear honey

For the salad

500g carrots, peeled and cut into ribbons with a Y-shaped vegetable peeler (be careful as you reach the centre to protect your fingertips)

1 small thumb of fresh root ginger, peeled and finely grated

1 small bunch of coriander, leaves picked

75g raw peanuts or cashew nuts, toasted and roughly chopped

1. First, make the dressing by whisking all the ingredients together in a small mixing bowl with a fork.

2. Place all the salad ingredients in a large salad bowl and toss to combine. Add the dressing and toss through the salad, then leave to sit for 15 minutes to allow the flavours to mingle before serving. Any remaining salad can be kept, covered, in the fridge for up to 3 days.

THE BEST OVEN CHIPS

The clever trick of soaking the spuds before cooking, and only seasoning them once they're done, is what takes these oven chips to the next level. These are especially good served with our Black Bean Veggie Burgers (see page 21).

SERVES 6–8

1.5kg floury potatoes, such as Maris Piper, peeled and cut into 1cm-thick sticks

Vegetable oil, for baking

Salt and freshly ground black pepper

1. Fill a large mixing bowl with cold water. Submerge the potato sticks in the water and leave to soak for 30 minutes.

2. Meanwhile, preheat the oven to 220°C/200°C fan/Gas Mark 7.

3. When the oven is up to temperature, coat the base of 2 large shallow roasting tins with a 1cm depth of vegetable oil (about 4 tablespoons in each tin is usually the right amount) and heat in the oven for 4 minutes.

4. Meanwhile, drain the potato sticks and pat dry between 2 layers of kitchen paper.

5. Remove the tins from the oven, divide the potato sticks between them and spread them out in an even layer in the hot oil, taking care as it may sizzle and spit, ensuring there is not too much overlap, as they won't crisp up if tightly packed together. Bake for 30–40 minutes, depending on the size of your chips, until they are crisp and golden, removing the tins from the oven 3 or 4 times during baking and giving them a good shake.

6. Remove from the oven and use a slotted spoon to transfer the chips to a large plate lined with kitchen paper.

7. Tip the chips into a large serving bowl, season with the salt and pepper and serve immediately.

BLITZED MINTY PEA MASH

Pies are carb-heavy affairs (if made correctly), so in place of the classic side of mashed potato, why not try a really good pea mash? It's a little lighter and perhaps even more delicious. This is great served with the Celeriac & Cheddar Crumble on page 109.

SERVES 4–6

2 tablespoons extra virgin olive oil

2 shallots, finely chopped

3 garlic cloves, finely chopped

700g frozen peas

100ml water

1 small bunch of mint, leaves picked and roughly chopped

25g unsalted butter

Juice of ½ lemon

Salt and freshly ground black pepper

1. Heat the olive oil in a large frying pan over a medium heat. Add the shallots with a pinch of salt and sauté for 4–5 minutes until soft and translucent. Then add the garlic and cook for a minute or so.

2. Stir the peas into the pan along with the measured water and cook for 7–8 minutes until they are tender but still bright green.

3. Tip the contents of the pan into a mixing bowl or a food processor and add the mint, butter and lemon juice. Blitz with a stick blender or the food processor until you have a bright green mash. Taste and season with salt and pepper. Serve while still warm.

HALLOUMI FRIES
WITH SWEET CHILLI & LIME YOGURT

Served hot from the pan, these crisp, cheesy fries are so good, they should probably come
with a warning. Just don't let them go cold – no one likes a rubbery chip.

SERVES 4–6 as a starter or side

2 × 250g packs halloumi cheese,
cut lengthways into 1cm-thick sticks

50g plain flour

1 egg

1 tablespoon white sesame seeds

1 tablespoon black sesame seeds

50g panko breadcrumbs (see tip)

Vegetable oil, for frying

Salt and freshly ground black pepper

Lime wedges, to serve

For the dip

150g Greek yogurt

3 tablespoons sweet chilli sauce

Grated zest and juice of 1 unwaxed lime

Salt and freshly ground black pepper

1. Pat the halloumi sticks dry between a couple of pieces of
   kitchen paper. Measure the flour out onto a plate, beat the
   egg in a wide bowl and mix the sesame seeds and breadcrumbs
   together on a separate plate. Roll the halloumi sticks in the
   flour, coating each side, then dip into the beaten egg and
   finally coat with the breadcrumb mixture – it's easiest to do
   this in a few batches.

2. Heat a 5mm depth of vegetable oil in a shallow frying pan
   over a medium–high heat until it reaches 180°C on a cooking
   thermometer or a piece of bread dropped into the hot oil
   browns in 20 seconds. Fry the halloumi sticks, in 3 batches,
   for about 3–4 minutes until golden and crisp on each side.
   Remove from the oil and drain on kitchen paper.

3. While the halloumi sticks are frying, prepare the dip by mixing
   the ingredients together in a small bowl, seasoning to taste with
   salt and pepper.

4. Serve the halloumi fries warm with lime wedges alongside for
   squeezing over and the yogurt dip.

TIP

PANKO BREADCRUMBS ARE A JAPANESE STYLE OF BREADCRUMB MADE FROM
CRUSTLESS, UNSEASONED WHITE BREAD, RESULTING IN A PARTICULARLY
CRISP COATING WHEN FRIED. IF PANKO BREADCRUMBS ARE TRICKY TO FIND,
USE ORDINARY FRESH OR DRIED WHITE BREADCRUMBS INSTEAD.

PURPLE SPROUTING BROCCOLI WITH HONEYED HALLOUMI

The earthy taste of purple broccoli pairs perfectly with the salty and sharp flavours from the halloumi and preserved lemon. I like to serve this as part of a midweek mezze alongside some dips, falafel and flatbreads.

SERVES 4 as a side

EQUIPMENT: griddle pan

400g purple sprouting broccoli, cut into 2cm pieces, thicker stalks halved lengthways

2 tablespoons white sesame seeds

3 tablespoons extra virgin olive oil

½ preserved lemon, flesh and pith discarded, rind finely chopped

1 tablespoon clear honey

250g pack halloumi cheese, cut into 1cm-thick slices

1. Place a griddle pan over a high heat to warm through – I usually heat mine for at least 5 minutes, otherwise there will be cooler spots and the food can stick.

2. Meanwhile, bring a large saucepan of water to the boil over a high heat. Plunge the broccoli into the boiling water and boil fast for 2 minutes. Drain the broccoli in a colander and then rinse under cold running water for at least 30 seconds to halt the cooking process and preserve the bright green colour of the broccoli spears and leaves.

3. Pat the broccoli dry on kitchen paper and cook, in batches, on the hot griddle pan. The trick here is not to add oil, otherwise the pan will smoke, and to avoid moving the broccoli around too much in the pan. After 3–4 minutes of cooking there should be distinct char marks on the broccoli. Keep the cooked batches of broccoli warm in a low oven, and once you have finished cooking the last batch, leave the griddle pan over a medium heat.

4. Toast the sesame seeds in a dry frying pan over a low heat for 3 minutes until golden and just starting to pop. Remove the pan from the heat and stir in the olive oil, preserved lemon and honey.

5. Add the halloumi slices to the griddle pan and cook for a minute on each side until striped with char marks and crispy.

6. Arrange the broccoli and halloumi on a warmed plate or large shallow bowl and pour over the sticky lemony dressing.

BRAISED LETTUCE & PEAS
WITH JERSEY ROYALS

The ingredients here may be humble, but the finished dish is anything but.
Served with a nice quiche, such as the Smoked Cheddar Tart with Walnut Crumb
on page 33, this would make a seriously satisfying lunch.

SERVES 6 as a side

750g baby Jersey Royal potatoes,
or other baby new potatoes

2 tablespoons olive oil

25g unsalted butter

2 banana shallots, finely chopped

2 garlic cloves, finely sliced

4 Baby Gem lettuces, each cut into
8 wedges

100ml vegetable stock

50ml white wine

400–500g fresh peas in the pod, shelled
to yield 100g

3 tablespoons double cream

1 small bunch of flat leaf parsley, leaves
picked and finely chopped

Salt and freshly ground black pepper

1. Bring a large saucepan of water to the boil, carefully lower in
   the potatoes and cook for 10–12 minutes or until just tender
   but still with a little resistance to a sharp knife. Drain in a
   colander and leave the potatoes to sit and let the steam escape
   for 2–3 minutes. Set aside.

2. While the potatoes are cooking, heat the olive oil in a large
   frying pan and add the butter. Once the butter has melted, add
   the shallots and sauté over a medium heat for 7–8 minutes. Stir
   in the garlic and cook for a minute. Add the lettuce wedges to
   the pan and cook, turning regularly, for a couple of minutes.

3. Pour the vegetable stock and wine into the pan, then add
   the peas. Bring to a gentle simmer and cook for a couple of
   minutes until the peas are just tender. Stir through the cream
   and parsley and season to taste with salt and pepper.

4. Tip the warm potatoes into a large shallow bowl, pour the braised
   lettuce and peas over the top and serve while still warm.

CARAMELIZED FENNEL WITH PANGRATTATO

Pangrattato – zhooshed-up crispy breadcrumbs to you and me – is a fab way to add flavour and texture to veggie dishes, and it works brilliantly as a topping for this rather sophisticated braised fennel.

SERVES 4–6 as a side

EQUIPMENT: 1 × 28cm non-stick frying pan

3 fennel bulbs, trimmed and halved from stalk end to root

75g unsalted butter

Generous pinch of salt

150ml white wine

1 tablespoon white wine vinegar

1 teaspoon light brown soft sugar

For the pangrattato

2 tablespoons olive oil

2 garlic cloves, finely chopped

50g coarse fresh or dried white breadcrumbs

5 sprigs of thyme, leaves picked

1 small bunch of flat leaf parsley, leaves picked and finely chopped

Grated zest of 1 unwaxed lemon

Salt and freshly ground black pepper

1. Bring a large saucepan of water to the boil. Plunge the fennel into the boiling water and cook for 6 minutes until soft to the prongs of a fork.

2. Melt the butter in a frying pan large enough to accommodate all the fennel. Add the salt to the butter and arrange the fennel, cut side down, in the pan.

3. Pour over the wine and vinegar, cover the pan with a lid or foil and cook over a high heat for 10 minutes without moving or shaking the pan.

4. While the fennel is cooking, turn your attention to the pangrattato. Heat the olive oil in a separate frying pan. Add the garlic, breadcrumbs, thyme and a pinch of salt and some pepper and cook over a medium heat, stirring continuously, for about 5 minutes until the breadcrumbs turn deep golden in colour. Remove the pan from the heat and stir in the parsley and lemon zest. Scrape the pangrattato onto a plate lined with kitchen paper to crisp up.

5. Remove the lid from the fennel pan and sprinkle the sugar around the base of the pan, rather than on top of the fennel. Cook for a further 2 minutes until the sugar has dissolved.

6. Arrange the fennel on a platter and pour over the remaining liquid from the pan (there may not be much, but it will have a powerful flavour). Sprinkle over some of the pangrattato and serve the remainder in a bowl for spooning over.

LEMONY ROASTIES
WITH CRISPY KALE

Crisp on the outside and fluffy in the middle: is there anything more pleasing than a proper roast potato? This recipe, with its crunchy kale and sticky roasted lemon, takes the Sunday classic up a notch.

SERVES 6–8 as a side

1.5kg floury potatoes, such as Maris Piper, peeled and each potato cut into 4–6 similar-sized pieces, depending on its size

100ml vegetable oil

2 lemons, halved

100g curly kale, washed, tough stalks removed and well dried

Salt and freshly ground black pepper

Flaky sea salt, to serve

1. Heat the oven to 220°C/200°C fan/Gas Mark 7.

2. Place the potatoes in a large saucepan, cover with cold water and add a generous pinch of salt. Bring the pan to the boil, then reduce the heat and simmer for 12–15 minutes until a sharp knife passes through the potatoes easily.

3. Drain the potatoes in a colander and leave them to sit and let the steam escape for a few minutes. Meanwhile, heat the vegetable oil in a large roasting tin in the oven for 3 minutes.

4. Remove the tin from the oven and spread the potatoes out in an even layer in the hot oil, taking care as it may sizzle and spit. Nestle the lemon halves among the potatoes and season well with salt and pepper. Roast for 40 minutes until the potatoes are crisp and golden, turning them with a spatula 2 or 3 times.

5. Scatter the kale over the potatoes and roast for 5 minutes until the kale crisps up and deepens in colour.

6. Remove from the oven and lift the vegetables onto a warmed serving platter with a slotted spoon to drain away any excess oil. Sprinkle over a little flaky sea salt before serving.

CARAMELIZED ONIONS WITH ORANGE & THYME

There's a tendency to underestimate the onion, but we do so at our peril. When given the treatment it deserves, it's up there with the best vegetables I know. These make a great accompaniment for the Beet Wellington on page 102 or your favourite Sunday roast.

SERVES 4–6 as a side

4 onions, peeled
100g unsalted butter
Zest and juice of 1 unwaxed orange
2 tablespoons balsamic vinegar
A few sprigs of thyme
Salt and freshly ground black pepper

1. Preheat the oven to 200°C/180°C fan/Gas Mark 6.

2. Halve the onions around their middles so that all the rings remain intact, then trim the top and the base of each so that they will sit flat whichever way up they are. Sit the onions in the roasting tin.

3. Melt the butter in a small frying pan. When it starts to foam, add the orange juice, vinegar and thyme and cook over a medium heat until the mixture looks emulsified. Season the butter mixture with salt and pepper, then pour over the onions.

4. Cover the tin tightly with foil and roast the onions for 1 hour, basting and turning them every 15 minutes.

5. Remove from the oven and reduce the temperature to 160°C/140°C fan/Gas Mark 3. Lift away the foil, baste the onions again and roast, uncovered, for a further 30 minutes. The onions are cooked when they are completely soft, yielding and brown all over. Serve hot, sprinkled with orange zest.

HONEY-ROASTED RADISHES

'OK, she's finally lost it,' I hear you cry. 'Roasted radishes?!?' Well, perhaps I have, but do try them. They're juicy and mellow, and the colour of the dish is just wonderful. These are great served with my Eat Your Greens Filo Pie on page 10.

SERVES 4 as a side

400g radishes, mixed colours and shapes, halved

3 tablespoons olive oil

Grated zest and juice of 1 unwaxed lemon

1 tablespoon clear honey

50g raw pistachio nuts, roughly chopped

100g goats' curd or ricotta cheese

5 sprigs of lemon thyme

Salt and freshly ground black pepper

1. Preheat the oven to 200°C/180°C fan/Gas Mark 6.

2. Place the radishes in a shallow roasting tin and drizzle over the olive oil. Add the lemon zest and juice and honey with a big pinch of salt and toss everything well to make sure that the olive oil, lemon and honey are coating every radish. Roast for 25 minutes, turning the radishes twice during this time.

3. Remove from the oven and turn the temperature up to 220°C/200°C fan/Gas Mark 7. Scatter the pistachios over the radishes. Crumble the goats' curd or ricotta into large chunks, about the size of a 50p coin (3cm), over the top, then pick the leaves from the lemon thyme sprigs and sprinkle these over too.

4. Roast the radishes for a further 10–12 minutes until they are starting to blister and the cheese is turning golden.

FENNEL & PARSNIP BOULANGÈRE

I like to think of this as the saintly sister of the slightly naughtier dauphinoise.
A mandoline is essential here, as the vegetables must be cut into paper-thin slices.
This goes well with the Cranberry & Porcini Nut Roast on page 89.

SERVES 8 as a side

EQUIPMENT: 1 rectangular ovenproof dish or shallow roasting tin, 20 × 30cm; mandoline slicer

100g unsalted butter, cut into small cubes

750g parsnips, peeled and finely sliced lengthways on the mandoline

2 fennel bulbs, trimmed and finely sliced on the mandoline

4 shallots, finely sliced

500g potatoes (about 3 large), peeled and finely sliced lengthways on the mandoline

400ml vegetable stock

Salt and freshly ground black pepper

1. Preheat the oven to 200°C/180°C fan/Gas Mark 6.

2. Grease the ovenproof dish or roasting tin lightly with a cube of the butter. Layer the parsnips, followed by the fennel, shallots and potatoes in the dish or tin, dotting the butter over each layer as you go and seasoning with salt and pepper, finishing with a layer of potatoes and a few cubes of butter on top.

3. Pour over the vegetable stock and cover the dish or tin tightly with foil. Bake for 45 minutes.

4. Remove from the oven and lift away the foil, then bake the boulangère, uncovered, for a further 45 minutes until golden on top and bubbling, and the vegetables are tender.

TIP

THIS CAN BE MADE A DAY AHEAD, COOLED COMPLETELY, COVERED AND REFRIGERATED, THEN REHEATED IN THE OVEN PREHEATED TO 180°C/160°C FAN/GAS MARK 4 FOR 30 MINUTES UNTIL PIPING HOT.

SWEET POTATO CAKES

These simple potato cakes make a handy addition to the weekly repertoire. I like to serve them alongside a green salad or, for those who aren't fully vegetarian, pieces of simply cooked fish.

MAKES 12 cakes

EQUIPMENT: Box grater

2 sweet potatoes (about 550g), peeled and cut into 7–8cm chunks

2 potatoes (about 500g), peeled and halved

2 teaspoons smoked paprika

4 tablespoons plain flour

Olive oil, for frying

Salt and freshly ground black pepper

To serve

Thick Greek yogurt

Freshly chopped coriander

Tomato Harissa Sauce (see page 211)

1. Bring a small saucepan of water to the boil, lower in the sweet potato and potato chunks and simmer for 10–12 minutes until just tender but still with a little resistance to a sharp knife.

2. Drain the potatoes in a colander and leave them to sit and let the steam escape for 2–3 minutes. Then grate on the coarse side of a box grater.

3. Mix the grated potato with the smoked paprika and flour in a large mixing bowl until well combined, then season really well with salt and pepper. Divide the mixture into 12 equal portions and, using your hands, shape each portion into a patty 6–7cm across.

4. Heat a good 1cm depth of olive oil in a large frying pan over a medium–high heat and fry the cakes, in batches, for 3–4 minutes on each side until they are brown and crisp. Place the cooked cakes on a baking sheet and keep warm in a low oven while you cook the remainder.

5. Serve with a generous spoonful of thick Greek yogurt, some fresh coriander and a spoonful of the Tomato Harissa Sauce.

SALT-BAKED CELERIAC WITH APPLE, KALE & BLUE CHEESE

Liberating a whole celeriac from its salty crust at the table is wonderful theatre.
But it's not just for show: the dough acts as vital insulation and makes for gentle, even cooking.

SERVES 6

400g strong white flour, plus a little extra for dusting

300g fine sea salt

4 egg whites

125ml water

1 celeriac (about 800g), washed and scrubbed (see tip)

200g curly kale, washed and tough stalks removed

Grated zest and juice of ½ unwaxed lemon

2 Granny Smith apples, cored and sliced into matchsticks

100g Stilton cheese, crumbled

75g walnuts

30g unsalted butter

30g golden caster sugar

Pinch of salt

Freshly ground black pepper

1. Preheat the oven to 200°C/180°C fan/Gas Mark 6.

2. Mix the flour and fine sea salt together in a large mixing bowl, then make a well in the centre. Add the egg whites and measured water to the well and use a fork to gradually mix the wet ingredients into the dry ingredients until a dough forms. Bring the dough together with your hands, wrap in cling film and chill in the fridge for 20 minutes.

3. Line a baking sheet with non-stick baking paper. Roll the dough out on a lightly floured surface to a 2cm-thick round, sit the celeriac in the centre and gather the dough up to encase it completely. Transfer the salt-encased celeriac to the lined baking sheet and bake for 1½–2 hours (depending on the size and age of the celeriac) until a skewer inserted into the celeriac pierces the salt casing and celeriac easily, and the vegetable feels tender.

4. While the celeriac is baking, place the kale in a large mixing bowl, sprinkle over the lemon zest and juice and use your hands to massage together until the kale is reduced by half in volume and the leaves have turned bright green. Mix through the apples and Stilton, season with pepper and set aside.

5. Have a sheet of non-stick baking paper ready on a surface nearby. Add the walnuts, butter and sugar to a large frying pan and cook over a medium heat, stirring continuously, for 8–10 minutes until the sugar has melted (it will clump together and darken in colour before it does so). Quickly stir in the salt, then transfer the walnuts to the sheet of baking paper and use a couple of spatulas to separate the nuts. Leave to cool and harden for 5 minutes.

6. Remove the celeriac from the oven and use a sharp knife to cut it into 6 wedges, discarding the salt casing. Divide the salad between 6 plates and serve a wedge of celeriac on top. Scatter over the candied walnuts and serve immediately.

TIP

USE A PASTRY BRUSH TO CLEAN INSIDE ANY KNOBBLY GROOVES ON THE CELERIAC.

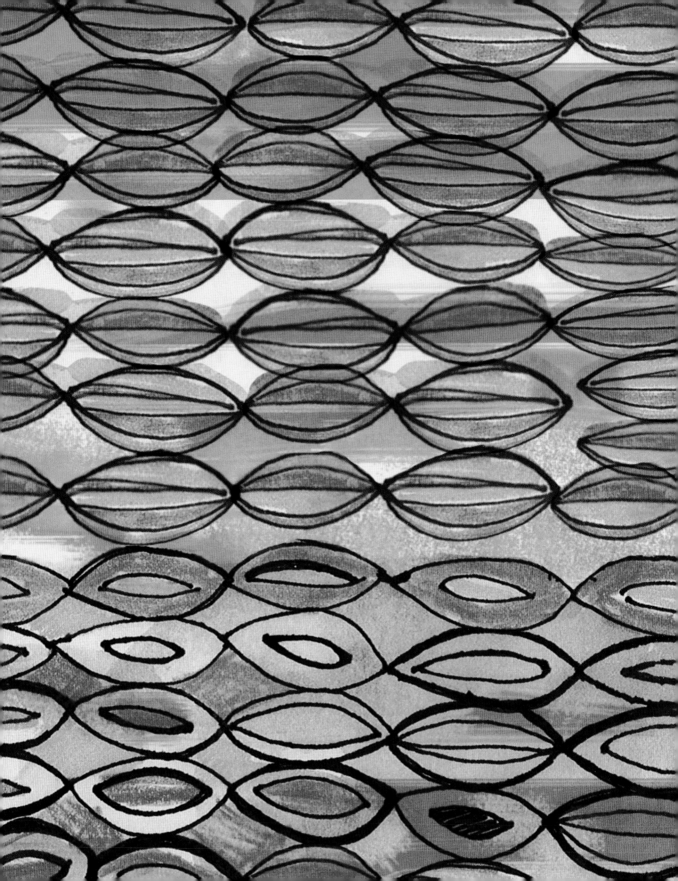

VEG ON THE GO

More and more of us are eating on the hop,
which is both great (it can be fun) and not so great
(often it's a bit unhealthy). But if you're feeling
organized, an afternoon of batch baking can arm you
with all the nibbles you'll need for the week ahead.

CHERRY TOMATO FOCACCIA

With its salty, faintly crisp crust and addictively chewy inside punctuated with incredible little cherry tomato flavour bombs, this rather pretty focaccia will pep up any picnic. It's delicious dunked into one of my dips (see pages 164–7) or, if you're feeling a bit 'wahey!', why not use it to make a superior sarnie?

SERVES 6

EQUIPMENT: 1 rectangular shallow roasting tin, 20 × 30cm

500g strong white flour, plus a little extra for dusting

7g fast-action dried yeast

10g fine sea salt

325ml warm water

2 tablespoons extra virgin olive oil, plus extra for oiling and drizzling

200g cherry tomatoes, halved

A few sprigs of rosemary, leaves picked

1 teaspoon flaky sea salt

1. Preheat the oven to 250°C/230°C fan or its highest setting.

2. Mix the flour, yeast, salt, measured warm water and olive oil together in a large mixing bowl to form a sticky dough. Turn the dough out on a floured surface and knead for about 10–15 minutes until it's smooth and silky, and bounces back when you poke it. Alternately, you can use a stand mixer fitted with the dough hook if you have one, but knead the dough for 5 minutes only.

3. Shape the dough into a ball and place in a lightly oiled bowl. Cover with a plastic bag or cling film and leave to rise in a warm place until it doubles in size – this should take about an hour.

4. Once the dough has risen, oil the roasting tin, then transfer the dough to the tin and shape it to fit the tin with an even thickness. Cover again with a plastic bag or cling film and leave the dough to rise for a further hour or until it has doubled in size again and is airy.

5. Push straight down with your fingers all over the dough to form holes almost reaching to the base of the tin. Push a tomato half and some rosemary leaves into each hole, then drizzle over some olive oil and sprinkle with the flaky sea salt.

6. Bake the focaccia on the middle shelf of the oven for 10 minutes, then reduce the oven temperature to 200°C/180°C fan/Gas Mark 6 and bake for a further 10 minutes.

7. Remove from the oven and drizzle more olive oil over the focaccia. Leave to cool for 10 minutes before slicing into squares in the tin.

SCOTCH VEG EGGS WITH TOMATO CHUTNEY

Shallow-frying these Scotch eggs gives a deliciously soft yolk, but for a healthier take you can instead bung them in the oven (200°C/180°C fan/Gas Mark 6 for 35–40 minutes) which, although hard-cooking the egg, will avoid using cooking oil. Use your leftover swede in my spicy Hidden Vegetable Pilaf on page 23 or Braised Roots with Orzo on page 56.

MAKES 6 Scotch eggs

6 small eggs, plus 2 medium eggs for the vegetable crust

1 potato (about 200g), unpeeled

6 tablespoons olive oil

1 red onion, finely chopped

2 garlic cloves, finely chopped

1 teaspoon dried thyme

2 teaspoons fennel seeds

¼ small swede (about 150g), peeled and grated

1 carrot (about 150g), peeled and grated

75g mature Cheddar cheese, grated

50g mixed seeds (I like pumpkin, sunflower and linseed), toasted

85g fresh or dried white breadcrumbs

30g plain flour

1 teaspoon pul biber (Turkish dried chilli flakes), or ¼ teaspoon dried chilli flakes

Salt and freshly ground black pepper

For the chutney

400g can chopped tomatoes

3 tablespoons capers in brine, drained and rinsed

1 tablespoon honey or maple syrup

2 tablespoons red wine vinegar

Salt and freshly ground black pepper

1. Place the small eggs in a large saucepan and cover with cold water. Bring to the boil over a high heat, and once boiling, set the timer for 3½ minutes. Meanwhile, half-fill a mixing bowl with cold water. When the egg cooking time is up, lift the eggs out of the pan and gently tap them on a hard surface to crack the shells. Lower them into the bowl of cold water until cooled (this makes them easier to shell). Carefully shell the eggs and set aside.

2. Place the unpeeled potato in a saucepan of cold water, bring to the boil and boil for 15–20 minutes or until a knife passes through it easily. Drain the potato and set aside until cool enough to handle, then peel away the skin, or trim it with a sharp knife if you prefer, and mash the potato with a fork in a large mixing bowl.

3. While the potato is cooking, heat 2 tablespoons of the olive oil in a frying pan, add the onion and gently sauté, stirring regularly, for about 5 minutes until soft and translucent. Add the garlic and cook, stirring, for 1 minute, then add the thyme and fennel seeds and cook for a further minute.

4. Divide the onion mixture in half, in the pan, then scrape one half into a small saucepan and set aside. Add the grated swede and carrot to the other half remaining in the pan and cook for 8 minutes until softened. Set aside to cool.

5. To make the chutney, add all the ingredients to the onion mixture in the small saucepan, seasoning well with salt and pepper. Bring to a gentle simmer, then reduce the heat and cook very gently, uncovered, for 25 minutes until the mixture is deep red and glossy. Taste and adjust the seasoning.

Continued overleaf >>

6. Tip the cooled grated vegetable mixture into the large bowl containing the mashed potato. Add the Cheddar, mixed seeds, 25g of the breadcrumbs, one of the remaining eggs, lightly beaten, and salt and pepper. Using your hands, turn the mixture to evenly combine. Then divide the mixture into 6 equal portions (I find it easiest to weigh out quantities of the mixture using kitchen scales to divide it up evenly).

7. Tip the flour onto a plate and sprinkle over some salt and pepper and the chilli flakes. Scatter the remaining breadcrumbs over a separate plate and beat the last remaining egg in a wide bowl.

8. Take one portion of the veggie mixture, flatten it out between the palms of your hands and then place a boiled egg in the centre. Carefully bring the edges of the veggie crust up around the egg and shape it into a ball. Roll the ball in the seasoned flour, then dip into the beaten egg and finally coat with breadcrumbs. Repeat with the remaining veggie mixture and boiled eggs.

9. Heat the remaining 4 tablespoons of olive oil in a large frying pan over a medium heat and fry the Scotch eggs, in 2 batches, for 8–10 minutes, turning regularly, until deep golden all over.

10. Transfer the Scotch eggs to a plate lined with kitchen paper and leave to cool a little. Serve either warm or cold with the chutney on the side for dipping.

MUSHROOM & PEARL BARLEY 'SAUSAGE' ROLLS

This is everything I look for in a veggie snack: deep umami flavours (Cheddar, white wine), heft (pearl barley, puff pastry) and heady top notes (thyme, mace, black onion/nigella seeds). And the porcini mushrooms, probably more than any other vegetable, give a pleasingly meaty texture. More often than not, I'll double the recipe and freeze half for a later date.

MAKES 6 rolls

EQUIPMENT: 1 × 28cm non-stick frying pan

20g dried porcini mushrooms

200ml warm water

25g pearl barley

250ml vegetable stock

40g unsalted butter, plus a little extra for greasing

2 shallots, finely diced

2 garlic cloves, crushed

400g chestnut mushrooms, finely diced

100ml dry white wine

1 teaspoon dried thyme

½ heaped teaspoon ground mace

¼ teaspoon ground cinnamon

50g mature Cheddar cheese, grated

1 egg, beaten, plus an extra 2 eggs to glaze

375g sheet of ready-rolled or ready-to-roll all-butter puff pastry, defrosted if frozen

A little plain flour, for dusting, if needed

1 teaspoon black onion (nigella) seeds

Salt and freshly ground black pepper

1. Cover the dried porcini with the measured warm water in a bowl and leave to soak for 30 minutes.

2. While the porcini is soaking, place the pearl barley in a saucepan, pour over the vegetable stock and cook according to the pack instructions.

3. Once the porcini soaking time is up, strain the porcini through a sieve over the pearl barley pan to catch the soaking liquid. Continue cooking the pearl barley until it is soft but still retains a little bite. Meanwhile, finely chop the soaked porcini and set aside.

4. Drain the cooked pearl barley and place in a mixing bowl.

5. Melt half the butter in a large frying pan, add the shallots and cook over a low heat for 10–12 minutes until soft and translucent. Add the garlic and cook for a further 2 minutes. Scrape the shallot mixture into the mixing bowl with the pearl barley and wipe out the pan with a piece of kitchen paper.

6. Return the pan to the heat and melt the remaining butter. Add the chestnut mushrooms with a pinch of salt and cook, stirring regularly with a wooden spoon, until all the liquid from the mushrooms has evaporated and the mushrooms are golden all over. Add the porcini and white wine to the pan and simmer until all the wine has been absorbed. Stir in the thyme, mace and cinnamon, and season well with salt and pepper.

7. Add the mushroom mixture to the pearl barley mixture in the mixing bowl along with the Cheddar. Taste and adjust the seasoning, then mix in the beaten egg.

Continued overleaf >>

8. Unroll the sheet of puff pastry, or if not ready-rolled, roll out on a lightly floured surface to a rectangle measuring about 24 × 33cm. Use a sharp knife to cut the pastry lengthways in half to make 2 rectangles measuring about 12 × 33cm. Brush one of the pastry rectangles all over with extra beaten egg. Form half the mushroom mixture into a long sausage shape slightly off-centre down the length of the rectangle, leaving a 2cm border on one side and a 6cm border on the other side. Lift the pastry from the 6cm edge over the mushroom mixture to meet the 2cm edge and roll over with your fingers to form a seal. Slip the long roll onto a tray lined with non-stick baking paper, making sure the seal is underneath. Chill in the fridge for at least 30 minutes. Repeat with the remaining pastry rectangle and mushroom mixture.

9. When ready to bake, preheat the oven to 200°C/180°C fan/ Gas Mark 6. Lightly grease a baking sheet with butter.

10. Remove the tray from the fridge and cut each roll into 3 equal lengths. Place on the greased baking sheet. Brush the tops of the rolls with beaten egg to glaze and scatter over the black onion seeds. Bake for 20–25 minutes until deep golden all over. Leave to cool on a wire rack and eat warm or at room temperature.

LEEK & POLENTA CAKE WITH WHIPPED FETA 'FROSTING'

A savoury cake? Have I completely lost the plot? Bear with me for a second. Think of this as a classic American cornbread, tarted up with sweet leeks, tangy feta cheese and a touch of spiky chilli. A good wedge of this, eaten alfresco with a glass of wine…I can think of worse things.

SERVES 8

EQUIPMENT: 1 × 23cm round springform cake tin

Vegetable oil, for oiling

50g unsalted butter

4 leeks, trimmed, cleaned and white and green parts finely chopped

2 green chillies, deseeded and finely chopped

150g quick-cook polenta

75g ground almonds

75g plain flour

2 teaspoons baking powder

125ml milk

200g Greek yogurt

3 eggs and 1 egg yolk, beaten together

200g can sweetcorn kernels, drained

75g feta cheese, crumbled

½ teaspoon pul biber (Turkish dried chilli flakes), or ½ teaspoon paprika

Grated zest of 1 unwaxed lemon

Salt and freshly ground black pepper

For the frosting

125g feta cheese, crumbled

50g Greek yogurt

1 garlic clove, crushed

1. Preheat the oven to 200°C/180°C fan/Gas Mark 6. Oil the cake tin and line the base with non-stick baking paper.

2. Melt the butter in a large frying pan. Add the leeks and season well with salt and pepper, then stir to coat in the melted butter and sauté over a medium heat for 15 minutes until completely soft and just starting to turn golden. Stir in the chillies and cook for 1 minute. Scrape three-quarters of the leek mixture into a small bowl, reserving the remainder for topping the cake at the end.

3. Mix the polenta and ground almonds together in a mixing bowl. Sift in the flour and baking powder, then mix in the milk, yogurt and whole egg and egg yolk mixture to form a batter. Fold through the larger quantity of leeks, the sweetcorn and feta, and season well.

4. Use a spatula to pour the batter into the prepared tin. Bake on the middle shelf of the oven for 30–35 minutes until a skewer inserted into the centre of the cake comes out clean.

5. While the cake is baking, make the frosting. Pulse the crumbled feta in a food processor until it resembles fine breadcrumbs. Add the yogurt and garlic to the processor and blitz on a high speed, scraping down the sides of the bowl a few times, for 1–2 minutes until the mixture thickens and is completely smooth. Transfer to a container, cover and chill in the fridge for at least 30 minutes until set.

6. Remove the cake from the oven and leave to cool in the tin for 10 minutes. Use a spatula to loosen the sides of the cake from the tin before releasing it. Leave to cool completely on a wire rack.

7. Spread the feta frosting over the top of the cooled cake and spoon over the reserved leeks. Finally, sprinkle over the pul biber or paprika and the lemon zest.

TIP

USE GLUTEN-FREE PLAIN FLOUR IF YOU ARE AVOIDING GLUTEN.

FOUR WAYS WITH KALE CRISPS

These kale crisps are habit-forming, no question, but would a kale addiction be such a bad thing? Perhaps it would if we were to eat nothing else, and there's a danger of that, so beware! It's the slightly seaweedy quality of these crisps that's especially appealing, and you can vary the flavourings according to your mood.

SERVES 4–6

100g curly kale, leaves stripped from the stalks, washed and well dried

1 tablespoon olive oil

¼ teaspoon fine sea salt

Salt and freshly ground black pepper

Flavouring options

• 1 teaspoon ground turmeric + grated zest of 1 unwaxed lemon

• 1 teaspoon dark miso paste + ½ teaspoon light soy sauce

• 25g Parmesan cheese, finely grated

• ½ teaspoon dried chilli flakes, or 1 teaspoon pul biber (Turkish dried chilli flakes)

1. Heat the oven to 120°C/100°C fan/Gas Mark ½.

2. Place the kale in a large mixing bowl, add your chosen flavouring ingredient(s) and the olive oil and fine sea salt and use your hands to massage together until you feel the kale start to soften between your fingers. Season with a little salt and pepper.

3. Carefully spread the kale out evenly on a baking tray and bake for 20 minutes.

4. Reduce the oven temperature to 90°C/70°C fan and bake for a further 20 minutes, then turn the oven off and leave the kale in the oven for 30 minutes to continue crisping up.

CORN & FETA MUFFINS

These Mexican-inspired muffins with their zingy feta, aromatic coriander and flavour pops of sweetcorn are a real lunchbox enlivener. Best of all, they are satisfyingly simple to make.

MAKES 12 muffins

EQUIPMENT: 1 × 12-hole muffin tin

3 eggs

100g fine cornmeal

75g plain flour, sifted

1 teaspoon baking powder, sifted

75ml milk

½ teaspoon salt

200g drained canned or frozen sweetcorn kernels, defrosted

1 red onion, very finely chopped

1 small bunch of coriander, leaves picked and chopped

100g feta cheese, crumbled

50g unsalted butter, melted, plus a little extra, if needed, for greasing

Freshly ground black pepper

1. Preheat the oven to 180°C/160°C fan/Gas Mark 4.

2. Beat the eggs with the cornmeal, flour, baking powder, milk and salt in a mixing bowl until you have a batter. Fold in the sweetcorn, red onion, coriander, feta and melted butter, then season well with pepper.

3. Grease the holes of the muffin tin with butter, or line with paper muffin cases. Divide the muffin batter between the holes and bake for 25–30 minutes until risen and a skewer inserted into the centre of a muffin comes out clean.

4. Remove the muffin tin from the oven and leave the muffins to cool in the tin for 10 minutes before transferring them to a wire rack to cool completely.

TIP

IF YOU STRUGGLE TO TRACK DOWN CORNMEAL, DON'T FRET, AS POLENTA WILL DO AN ADMIRABLE JOB. YOUR MUFFINS WILL BE SLIGHTLY COARSER IN TEXTURE, BUT NO LESS DELICIOUS FOR IT.

QUINOA-STUFFED PEPPERS

There's a lot of hype about quinoa, but I have to say, I'm a total convert.
Its distinctive nutty taste works brilliantly against the smoky paprika and aromatic fennel
in these super-savoury stuffed peppers. Oh, and if you're cooking your own rather than using
ready-cooked quinoa, try toasting it in the pan before adding your liquid (see page 34),
which will bring out even more nuttiness.

SERVES 4

4 red, orange or yellow peppers, or a mixture, halved from stalk end to base, cored and deseeded

Olive oil, for sautéing

1 white onion, finely diced

2 carrots, finely diced

1 fennel bulb, trimmed and finely diced

1 teaspoon hot smoked or sweet smoked paprika (sweet smoked isn't as spicy)

50g quinoa, cooked according to the pack instructions, or 125g ready-cooked quinoa

100g cherry tomatoes, roughly chopped

75g pine nuts, toasted

50g pitted black olives, roughly chopped

1 bunch of flat leaf parsley, leaves picked and finely chopped, plus extra to garnish

Salt and freshly ground black pepper

1. Preheat the oven to 200°C/180°C fan/Gas Mark 6.

2. Arrange the peppers, cut side up, in a shallow roasting tin. Sprinkle over some salt and pepper and bake for 15 minutes. Remove from the oven and leave to cool.

3. Meanwhile, heat enough olive oil to coat the base of a frying pan over a medium heat. Add the onion, carrots and fennel to the pan with a pinch of salt and sauté, stirring regularly, for 15 minutes until soft, sweet and translucent and starting to brown in places. Stir in the smoked or sweet paprika and toast for a minute or so.

4. Tip the sautéed vegetable mixture into a mixing bowl and stir in all the remaining ingredients. Taste and adjust the seasoning.

5. Divide the quinoa and vegetable mixture between the pepper halves and bake for 30–35 minutes until the peppers are soft to the point of a knife.

6. Remove from the oven and leave the peppers to cool in the tin for 10 minutes, which helps the filling to firm up, before lifting them out and serving garnished with extra chopped parsley.

TIP

ANY EXTRA QUINOA STUFFING CAN BE SPOONED ONTO A BAKED POTATO OR MIXED WITH SOME SALAD LEAVES FOR A QUICK, HEALTHY LUNCH.

SPICED BUTTERMILK SCONE WITH RED ONION CHUTNEY

The traditional scone is spruced up here with the addition of subtle spices and red onion chutney. This is designed as a generous tear 'n' share version for plonking in the middle of the table or picnic blanket and serving for lunch.

SERVES 4–6

EQUIPMENT: 1 × 20cm round cake tin

250g wholemeal flour, plus a little extra for dusting

3 teaspoons baking powder

60g unsalted butter, cut into 1cm cubes

90g mature Cheddar cheese, grated

2 teaspoons garam masala

20g coriander, roughly chopped

1 green chilli, deseeded and finely chopped

80ml buttermilk

1 large egg, plus 1 medium egg yolk

Butter, to serve

For the chutney

4 red onions, finely chopped

125ml cider vinegar

75g light brown soft sugar

1 tablespoon tamarind paste

½ teaspoon black mustard seeds

1. Start by making the chutney. Place the onions, vinegar and sugar in a large saucepan over a high heat, bring to a simmer and cook for 10 minutes. Reduce the heat and cook very gently, uncovered, for 1 hour, stirring regularly to prevent the mixture from catching on the base of the pan. If the mixture becomes too dry, stir through a little hot water as needed. You are looking for the consistency to change from slightly watery to syrupy. When the chutney is done, just before removing the pan from the heat, stir through the tamarind paste and black mustard seeds. Set aside and keep warm.

2. Preheat the oven to 200°C/180°C fan/Gas Mark 6. Lightly flour the cake tin.

3. Sift the flour and baking powder into a mixing bowl. Add the butter and rub in with your fingertips until it resembles fine breadcrumbs. Stir in the Cheddar and garam masala, followed by the coriander and chilli.

4. Lightly beat the buttermilk and whole egg and egg yolk together in a small mixing bowl. Add to the flour mixture and beat until you have a smooth dough.

5. Turn the dough out onto a lightly floured surface and shape into a 15cm round. Flour the handle of a wooden spoon and make 3 intersecting indentations across the dough round to divide it up into 6 equal-sized wedges by pushing the handle roughly halfway down into the dough, being careful not to cut all the way through.

6. Transfer the scone to the floured cake tin and bake for 18–20 minutes until risen, golden and cooked through. Remove from the oven and leave to cool in the tin for 15 minutes before serving warm with butter and chutney.

TIP

IF YOU DON'T EAT ALL THE CHUTNEY IMMEDIATELY, TRANSFER IT TO A STERILIZED GLASS JAR, PLACE A GREASEPROOF PAPER DISC ON TOP OF THE CHUTNEY AND SEAL THE JAR. STORE IN THE FRIDGE FOR UP TO 6 WEEKS.

SALTED ALMOND, SAGE & PARMESAN BISCOTTI

Twice baked, these crisp savoury biscotti are just the thing served with an ice-cold aperitivo, slivers of hard cheese and some whipped soft cheese for dunking.

MAKES 12 biscotti

185g plain flour, plus a little extra for dusting

½ teaspoon baking powder

Pinch of salt

25g Parmesan cheese, finely grated

6 sage leaves, finely chopped

25g ground almonds

50g whole unblanched almonds

2 large eggs, lightly beaten

1. Preheat the oven to 180°C/160°C fan/Gas Mark 4. Line a baking sheet with non-stick baking paper.

2. Sift the flour, baking powder and salt into a large mixing bowl, add the Parmesan, sage and ground and whole almonds and give the ingredients a good mix.

3. Add the beaten eggs to the dry ingredients and mix first with a wooden spoon and then use your hands to bring the mixture together to form a smooth dough.

4. Turn the dough out on a lightly floured surface and, using your hands again, roll it into a log measuring about 24 × 4cm. Place the log on the lined baking sheet and bake on the middle shelf of the oven for 30 minutes. Remove from the oven and allow to cool. Reduce the oven temperature to 150°C/130°C fan/ Gas Mark 2.

5. Transfer the baked log to a board and use a serrated knife to cut it carefully and gently on a slight diagonal into 12 slices about 1cm thick. Arrange the slices in a single layer on the lined baking sheet and bake for a further 30 minutes, turning over halfway through that time, until pale gold in colour on both sides and crisp.

6. Remove from the oven and transfer the biscotti to a wire rack to cool completely before storing in an airtight container. They will keep for up to 2 weeks.

TIP

SWAP THE ALMONDS FOR WALNUTS OR HAZELNUTS IF THEY'RE MORE TO YOUR TASTE.

POTATO, PARSNIP & PARSLEY FARLS

A farl is simply a flattish potato scone cooked in a frying pan on the hob. I've introduced parsnip to the traditional recipe for a touch of earthy sweetness, along with some finely chopped parsley, which lifts the flavours and makes for a handsome-looking finished farl. These work brilliantly in any fry-up scenario, being particularly firm friends with eggs, whether fried or poached.

MAKES 4 farls

1 floury potato, such as Maris Piper (250g peeled weight), peeled and chopped into 4 equal-sized pieces

1 parsnip (220g peeled weight), peeled and chopped into 4 equal-sized pieces

30g unsalted butter, melted

50g plain flour

½ teaspoon baking powder

2 tablespoons finely chopped flat leaf parsley

Salt and freshly ground black pepper

1. Bring a saucepan of water to the boil, lower in the potato and parsnip pieces and boil for 20 minutes or until a sharp knife passes through them easily. Drain and return to the pan. Add the melted butter and use a potato masher to mash the root vegetables with the butter. Season well with salt and pepper, then set aside to steam dry for 5 minutes.

2. Using a wooden spoon, stir the flour, baking powder and parsley into the mash and mix together until well incorporated.

3. Remove the root vegetable 'dough' from the pan and, using your hands, flatten the dough to form a flat disc about 18–20cm across. Cut the disc into quarters.

4. Heat a dry non-stick frying pan over a medium heat. Add the farls to the hot pan and cook for 4 minutes, then carefully turn them and cook on the other side for 4 minutes. Serve immediately.

RAINBOW VEG ROLLS WITH PEANUT DIPPING SAUCE

Once everything's chopped, this recipe is a total doddle. You could even serve the filling ingredients next to a pile of rice paper wrappers and invite your guests to make their own. Just remember to have a bowl of hot water on the table, as each wrapper will need a quick bath before it's ready to roll.

MAKES ABOUT 24 veg rolls

100g dried cellophane noodles

2 teaspoons sesame oil

1 pack rice paper wrappers

1 large bunch of coriander, leaves picked

1 small bunch of mint, leaves picked

½ cucumber, halved and seeds scraped out with the tip of a teaspoon, then cut into very thin strips

2 carrots, peeled and cut into very thin strips

1 red pepper, cored, deseeded and cut into very thin strips

6 radishes, very thinly sliced

5–6 spring onions, cut into very thin strips

1 avocado, stoned, peeled and cut into very thin strips

For the peanut sauce

4 tablespoons smooth or chunky peanut butter

4 tablespoons rice vinegar

2 tablespoons light soy sauce

1 tablespoon light brown soft sugar

Pinch of dried chilli flakes

1. Start by making the peanut sauce. Measure all the ingredients into a small saucepan, place over a low heat and warm through, stirring continuously, until the mixture just begins to bubble. Remove from the heat and set aside.

2. Place the noodles in a heatproof bowl, pour over boiling water to cover and leave to soak for 10 minutes until rehydrated. Drain well and return to the dried-out bowl. Drizzle over the sesame oil and toss the noodles to evenly coat.

3. Fill a separate bowl with hot water. Take a rice paper wrapper and dip in the hot water for about 5 seconds until soft and pliable – they really don't need long.

4. Lay the wrapper on a board and, working quickly, arrange some of the herb leaves down the centre of the wrapper. Then take a little of each of the thinly cut vegetables to create a neat pile in the centre of the wrapper. Finally, place a small bundle of rehydrated noodles on the very top of the veg. Fold in the edges of the wrapper over the veggies and then roll up.

5. Repeat with the remaining wrappers, herbs, veg and noodles.

6. Cut each roll in half to expose the pretty rainbow colours of the vegetables and serve with the warm peanut sauce.

CARROT & DATE ENERGY BALLS

Ah, that perennial problem of the afternoon slump. I don't think any of us is immune from it, especially if lunch has been a carb-heavy affair. As easy – and tempting – as it is to reach for a chocolate bar, it's just as easy to grab one of these energy balls. My approach is to rustle up a batch or two of these on a weekend and store them in the fridge for the coming week.

MAKES 15 balls

50g jumbo oats

50g mixed nuts, toasted (I like almonds, hazelnuts and walnuts)

150g carrot, peeled and finely grated

300g pitted Medjool dates, roughly chopped

1 teaspoon ground cinnamon

½ teaspoon fine sea salt

1. Pulse the jumbo oats in a food processor a few times to break them down.

2. Add the nuts and pulse again until a rough flour-like texture forms, but not so much that the nuts and oats are completely fine (you still want some texture).

3. Add the remaining ingredients and pulse again until you have a thick dough that comes together easily and holds its shape when you pinch it between your fingers.

4. Line a tray with non-stick baking paper. Using wet hands, roll the dough into 15 golf ball-sized balls. Transfer to the lined tray and chill in the fridge for 4 hours until firm. Store in an airtight container in the fridge for up to a week.

FRUIT ROLL-UPS

This is essentially a recipe for fruit 'leather', but as we're in full-on veggie mode,
we won't dwell on that word. You can use any fruit you like to make these roll-ups
(see the photograph on page 161) – in fact, they're a fantastic way to make the most of
a seasonal glut. However, avoid any temptation to use frozen fruit, as it tends not to set as
well as fresh. These are astonishingly easy to make, so don't be put off by the long cooking
time because the fruit is simply left to bake in the oven overnight.

MAKES 10 roll-ups

EQUIPMENT:
1 rectangular shallow
roasting tin, 20 × 30cm

Sunflower oil, for oiling
500g mixed fresh fruit,
washed

1. Preheat the oven to 70°C/50°C fan. Lightly oil the roasting tin and line with lightly oiled non-stick baking paper.

2. Trim any larger pieces of fruit and remove any leaves, stones or pips and stalks. Place the fruit in a saucepan and cover the pan with a lid. Cook gently over a low heat for 10 minutes or until the fruit is soft but not yet broken down.

3. Transfer the fruit to a blender or food processor and blitz for 3 minutes or until very smooth. Pour the fruit purée into the lined tin and leave to bake overnight – 12–15 hours is usually long enough for the fruit to be dry to the touch and leathery, although some fruit will take less time.

4. Remove the tin from the oven and use sharp scissors to cut the fruit 'leather' into 3cm-wide strips across the tin from one long side to the other to make 10 strips. Roll each strip up into a snail-shell shape. Store the fruit roll-ups in an airtight container for up to 3 weeks.

TIP

GOOD COMBOS OF FRUIT INCLUDE STRAWBERRIES AND BLACKCURRANTS, APPLES AND
BLACKBERRIES, AND GREEN GRAPES AND KIWIS.

QUICK YOGURT FLATBREADS WITH VEGGIE DIPS

Each of these three delicious dips serves 4–6 people, and can be made in advance and stored in the fridge, tightly covered with cling film, for up to three days. The flatbreads can also be made and cooked ahead, then wrapped loosely in foil and reheated in the oven.

QUICK YOGURT FLATBREADS

I reckon you could probably make these simple flatbreads in the time it would take to run to the corner shop and back. And they really are so much tastier than even the best shop-bought pitta. As well as being great with the dips, they go beautifully with my Roasted Cauliflower & Chickpea Curry on page 22.

MAKES 8 flatbreads

EQUIPMENT: griddle pan or frying pan

200g natural yogurt

200g strong white flour, plus a little extra for dusting

1 teaspoon baking powder

½ teaspoon fine sea salt

1. Place all the ingredients in a mixing bowl and mix together with a wooden spoon until they come together to form a dough.

2. Turn the dough out on a lightly floured surface and knead briefly for a minute or so. This isn't a traditional bread recipe, so you don't want to knead the dough too much to develop the gluten in the flour.

3. Heat a griddle pan or frying pan over a high heat. Meanwhile, using your hands, roll the dough into 8 golf ball-sized balls, then use a rolling pin to roll out each ball on a lightly floured surface into a 5mm-thick round.

4. Cook the flatbreads, one at a time, in the hot pan for 2–3 minutes on each side until puffed up and charred. Keep warm, wrapped in a clean tea towel.

5. Serve the flatbreads warm on a board with the dips arranged in the centre.

TIP

DON'T BE PUT OFF BY MAKING YOUR OWN FLATBREADS, AS THIS RECIPE DOESN'T REQUIRE MUCH KNEADING OR RESTING TIME.

BEETROOT MUHAMMARA

Watch out hummus, there's a new dip in town. Well, new to me at least, but no doubt in the Middle East they've been savvy to the joys of muhammara for a very long time. The traditional version is made with red peppers, but my crimson take on this Syrian classic uses earthy beetroot – one of my favourite vegetables.

SERVES 4–6

400g raw, unpeeled beetroot (6 small beetroot or 2 large)

1 tablespoon balsamic vinegar

5 tablespoons extra virgin olive oil

2 garlic cloves, finely chopped

1 tablespoon cumin seeds, toasted and roughly ground using a pestle and mortar

1 tablespoon pul biber (Turkish dried chilli flakes), or 1 teaspoon dried chilli flakes

2 tablespoons pomegranate molasses, or balsamic vinegar sweetened with ½ teaspoon clear honey

1 teaspoon paprika

150g walnuts, toasted and roughly chopped

75–100ml water

Salt and freshly ground black pepper

A little crumbled feta cheese, to garnish

1. Preheat your oven to 200°C/180°C fan/Gas Mark 6.

2. Scrub the beetroot well, then place in a small shallow roasting tin with the vinegar, 1 tablespoon of the olive oil and some salt and pepper. Rub the beetroot all over with the oil, then cover the tin with foil and bake for 1–1½ hours, depending on the size of your beetroot – it should be soft to the point of a knife.

3. Remove from the oven, lift away the foil and leave the beetroot to cool for at least 10 minutes before rubbing off their skins.

4. Roughly chop the beetroot, then add to a food processor with the garlic and pulse to combine. Add all the other ingredients except the remaining olive oil, season with a generous pinch of salt, and pulse again with enough of the measured water to achieve a much smoother consistency but still with a little texture.

5. Taste and adjust the seasoning, then stir through the remaining 4 tablespoons of olive oil. Serve in a bowl with a little feta sprinkled over to garnish.

RED PEPPER ROMESCO

My gosh, the Catalans are good at sauces. As if inventing the mighty allioli wasn't enough,
they managed to do the double with their equally stunning romesco: a sweet, smoky, nutty dip with
a subtle but crucial kick. It goes brilliantly with just about anything, from flatbreads to fish.

SERVES 4-6

3 red peppers

50g whole blanched almonds, toasted

1 tomato or 4 cherry tomatoes, roughly
chopped

2 slices of stale white bread – sourdough
is best

1 tablespoon sherry or balsamic vinegar

1 garlic clove, finely chopped

1 teaspoon smoked paprika

1 small dried red chilli, or ½ teaspoon
dried chilli flakes

1 tablespoon tomato purée

1 small bunch of flat leaf parsley, leaves
picked and roughly chopped

1 teaspoon fennel seeds, lightly toasted

6 tablespoons olive oil, plus extra if needed

Salt and freshly ground black pepper

1. Preheat the oven to 200°C/180°C fan/Gas Mark 6. Place the
   peppers in a shallow roasting tin or ovenproof dish without any
   oil. Bake for 30 minutes until the skins have started to wrinkle
   and char in places.

2. When the peppers have been roasting for 18 minutes, spread
   the almonds out on a baking tray in a single even layer, place
   on another shelf of the oven and roast until they are golden all
   over, by which time the peppers should be done as well.

3. Remove the peppers and almonds from the oven. Transfer the
   peppers to a glass or plastic bowl, cover the bowl with cling
   film and leave until cool enough to handle.

4. Add the almonds to a mixing bowl with all the remaining
   ingredients, seasoning with salt and pepper.

5. When the peppers are cool enough, peel away the skins and
   discard the seeds, then add the flesh to the mixing bowl.
   Using a stick blender or a food processor, blitz until you have
   a spoonable, chunky consistency, adding more oil and/or a
   splash of water to loosen if needed.

BROAD BEAN & MINT DIP

This zingy dip makes great use of the humble frozen broad bean – a criminally underrated veggie in my view. Releasing them from their skins before blitzing will give the finished dip a striking green colour, and the toasted almonds lend both smokiness and heft. This is also very good with crudités.

SERVES 4–6

500g frozen broad beans

Juice of 1 small lemon

2 garlic cloves, roughly chopped

50g pecorino cheese, finely chopped

25g whole blanched almonds, toasted and chopped

½ small bunch of dill, leaves picked

½ small bunch of mint, leaves picked and any smaller leaves reserved to garnish

4 tablespoons olive oil

Salt and freshly ground black pepper

1. Fill a kettle with water and bring to the boil. Tip the broad beans into a large, heatproof bowl, pour over the boiling water to cover and leave to soak for 5 minutes.

2. Drain the beans, and when cool enough to handle, slip them out of their skins to reveal the bright green beans inside and add to a food processor.

3. Add all the remaining ingredients and pulse until a salsa-like consistency forms. Taste and season with salt and pepper.

TIP

THE TIME-CONSUMING BUT WORTHWHILE TASK OF SKINNING THE BROAD BEANS IS A VERY GOOD ONE FOR CHILDREN TO DO.

BENTO BOX SALAD

Too often salads don't travel well, arriving at the destination as a wilted, diminished version of their former selves. Here I've chosen sturdy ingredients, mostly to be found at your local corner shop, which pull together well to make a delicious salad that could form the backbone of any picnic or lunch to go.

SERVES 4

200g couscous

250ml vegetable stock

Juice of 1 lemon

A glug of olive oil

1 large onion, finely chopped

4 garlic cloves, sliced

1 teaspoon ground coriander

200g drained sun-dried tomatoes in oil, quartered

For the salad

½ cucumber

1 large, ripe but firm avocado

150g baby plum tomatoes, halved

3 spring onions, white and light green parts sliced on the diagonal

1 small bunch of parsley, leaves picked and chopped

Grated zest and juice of 1 unwaxed lemon

1. Start by preparing the couscous. Heat a large non-stick frying pan over a medium heat, add the couscous and gently toast for 5–7 minutes or until the grains are golden brown in colour, shaking the pan occasionally. Tip into a large heatproof bowl.

2. Bring the vegetable stock to the boil in a saucepan, then pour over the couscous along with the lemon juice and stir well. Cover with a plate or baking sheet and set aside for 10 minutes until all the liquid has been absorbed, then fluff the couscous up with a fork.

3. Wipe the frying pan clean of any couscous, add the olive oil and set the pan over a medium–high heat. Add the onion and cook for about 4–5 minutes until soft and brown. Stir in the garlic and coriander, reduce the heat and cook for a minute.

4. Remove the pan from the heat and leave the onion mixture to cool slightly before stirring into the couscous with the sun-dried tomatoes.

5. While the onion mixture is cooking and cooling, prepare the salad. Halve the cucumber lengthways and use the tip of a teaspoon to scrape out the soft seeds from the centre of each half. Then cut the cucumber halves into thin, crescent-shaped slices. Place in a large mixing bowl. Halve the avocado and remove the stone, then peel and cut the flesh into 1–2cm cubes. Add to the bowl with the tomatoes, spring onions, parsley, lemon zest and juice, and gently toss to combine.

6. Pile the couscous into a dish or food storage container, make a well in the centre and fill with the salad. Cover or seal and then either serve just as it is or toss the couscous and salad together.

ROASTED VEGETABLE PICNIC LOAF

This show-stopping sarnie loaf has all the drama of a pie without any of the faff that comes with making your own pastry. The best sort of loaf to use is a French boule, but any large round loaf will do the job. Perfect for transporting to picnics, all that's needed is a bread knife to carve the loaf up.

SERVES 8

2 red and 2 yellow peppers, cored, deseeded and quartered

2 courgettes, cut into 5mm–1cm-thick slices on the diagonal

125g cherry tomatoes, halved horizontally

2–3 tablespoons olive oil

1 large French boule loaf, about 25cm in diameter and 800g in weight

5 eggs

250ml double cream

125g mature Cheddar cheese, grated

20g basil leaves, roughly chopped

Salt and freshly ground black pepper

1. Preheat the oven to 200°C/180°C fan/Gas Mark 6. Divide the pepper quarters and courgette slices between 2 shallow roasting tins, and place the tomatoes in a third roasting tin. Season everything with salt and pepper and toss in the olive oil. Spread the vegetables out evenly in a single layer, ensuring there is little overlap – this helps them to roast rather than steam.

2. Roast all the vegetables for 15 minutes, then remove the tomatoes from the oven. Turn the peppers and courgettes over and roast for a further 20 minutes. Remove from the oven and set aside to cool slightly. Reduce the oven temperature to 160°C/140°C fan/Gas Mark 3.

3. Cut about one-third off the top of your loaf to leave a depth of 6–7.5cm for the filling. Hollow out the loaf, removing 90 per cent of the soft crumb inside, but be careful not make the outer shell too thin, otherwise it might not be strong enough to hold the filling; a thickness of about 1cm is perfect.

4. Crack the eggs into a mixing bowl and lightly beat with a fork. Pour in the cream and add two-thirds of the Cheddar and basil. Season heavily with salt and pepper.

5. Arrange the roasted courgette slices in an even layer in the base of the loaf. Sprinkle over a little of the reserved basil and top with the roasted peppers. Pour over the egg mixture – there should be about a 2.5cm clearance between the top of your filling mixture and the lip of the loaf. Scatter over the roasted tomatoes, dress the top of the filling with the remaining Cheddar and basil and season well.

6. Place the loaf on a baking sheet and bake on the middle shelf of the oven for 1–1¼ hours until the filling is firm to the touch.

7. Turn the oven off and leave the loaf to cool in the oven for at least another hour, but overnight is best. Remove from the oven and slice into wedges to serve.

TIP

DON'T WASTE THE BREAD FROM THE MIDDLE OF THE LOAF – USE IT TO MAKE CROUTONS OR BREADCRUMBS, OR MY MOZZARELLA, TOMATO & GREEN OLIVE BREAD SALAD ON PAGE 44.

SWEET TREATS

A whole chapter on desserts? In a veggie cookbook?
Isn't that rather cheeky? Well, maybe. In my defence,
all the recipes that follow let veg or fruit take centre
stage. And anyway, what right-minded person
doesn't love a good pud?

ORANGE & ROSEMARY UPSIDE-DOWN CAKE

This recipe is unashamedly British in its simplicity. Not that there's anything humdrum about it – quite the contrary. The rosemary and orange work together to create the most incredible aroma.

SERVES 8–10

EQUIPMENT: 1 × 23cm round springform cake tin

3 unwaxed oranges

250g caster sugar

150g unsalted butter, softened

3 eggs, separated

1 teaspoon vanilla paste

2 sprigs of rosemary, leaves picked and roughly chopped

100g ground almonds

100g polenta

1½ teaspoons baking powder

Pinch of salt

1. Preheat the oven to 180°C/160°C fan/Gas Mark 4. Line the base and sides of the cake tin with non-stick baking paper.

2. Place one of the oranges in a deep saucepan, cover with water and bring to the boil. Boil for an hour, topping the water up occasionally to ensure that the orange remains covered. Remove the pan from the heat and leave to cool.

3. Using a serrated knife, cut the remaining 2 oranges horizontally into 5mm-thick slices, lifting out any pips as you go, and reserve any juicy ends. Place the orange slices in a frying pan and scatter 100g of the sugar over the top. Squeeze over any juice from the reserved orange ends and cook the orange slices over a high heat for 10 minutes, turning occasionally with a slotted spoon, at which point they should start to resemble candied fruit in a sticky syrup. Remove the pan from the heat. Arrange the orange slices evenly across the base of the lined cake tin – don't worry if there is a bit of overlap. Pour over the sugar syrup from the frying pan and set aside.

4. Beat the butter with the remaining 150g sugar in a stand mixer fitted with the paddle attachment or in a large mixing bowl with an electric whisk until light and fluffy. Then beat in the egg yolks and vanilla paste.

5. When the boiled orange has cooled, cut it in half around the middle and remove any visible pips. Add the halves to a food processor with the rosemary leaves and blitz to a smooth pulp with a little texture remaining. Fold the orange mixture through the cake batter, followed by the ground almonds, polenta, baking powder and salt.

6. Whisk the egg whites in the stand mixer fitted with the whisk attachment or in a mixing bowl with the cleaned electric whisk until stiff peaks form, then fold them through the cake batter with a spatula. Scrape the batter into the prepared tin and level the surface.

7. Bake on the middle shelf of the oven for 35–40 minutes until a skewer inserted into the centre of the cake comes out clean. Remove from the oven and leave to cool in the tin for at least 20 minutes before carefully inverting onto a large round plate or platter. Leave to cool completely before slicing.

PISTACHIO & APRICOT BAKLAVA

Baklava may sound exotic and mysterious, conjuring images of souks piled high with nuts and spices, but in reality it's extremely straightforward to make. Like most sweetmeats, it's great with a pot of tea. Alternatively, if you're feeling a little more adventurous, try serving it after a Middle Eastern-style main course, like my Stuffed Bulgur Aubergine with Chermoula on page 74.

MAKES ABOUT 36 pieces

EQUIPMENT: 1 rectangular baking tin, 20 × 30cm

350g raw pistachio nuts

130g caster sugar

Seeds from 10 green cardamom pods (pods discarded)

¼ teaspoon ground cinnamon

100g ready-to-eat dried apricots

Small pinch of salt

150g unsalted butter, melted

12 sheets of filo pastry (usually 2 packs of filo), defrosted if frozen and kept covered in a clean tea towel if frozen

150g clear honey

Grated zest and juice of 1 unwaxed lemon

1. Preheat the oven to 160°C/140°C fan/Gas Mark 3.

2. Add the pistachios, 2 tablespoons of the sugar, the spices, apricots and salt to a food processor and pulse until the mixture resembles coarse breadcrumbs, being careful to stop pulsing before it turns into a thick paste.

3. Brush the sides of the baking tin with melted butter, then lay a sheet of filo across the base. Fold any overhanging edges of pastry in to form a neat rectangle that nestles inside the tin's sides, then brush the top of the pastry with butter. Repeat with 3 more sheets of filo, brushing with melted butter as you go. Spread half the nut mixture over the fourth sheet of filo so that it's evenly distributed up to the sides of the tin. Lay 4 more sheets of filo over the nut mixture, brushing each one with melted butter, then spread the remaining nut mixture over the fourth sheet of filo. Finish the baklava with the remaining 4 sheets of filo, each brushed with butter.

4. Cut the baklava into diamonds or squares about the size of a passport photo, slicing right through to the base of the tin, and bake for 50 minutes until puffed up and golden on top.

5. While the baklava is baking, make the syrup. Place the remaining sugar with the honey and lemon zest and juice in a small saucepan. Cook over a low heat until the sugar has melted and the syrup has turned from golden to a deep caramel colour.

6. Remove the baklava from the oven and immediately pour over the syrup (warm it through to make it runny if it has cooled down and hardened). Leave the baklava to cool in the tin for 15 minutes before transferring to a plate to serve. It will keep in an airtight container for up to a week.

PLUM COBBLER

It's hard to think of a better use for a bowl of ripe plums than this ever-so-comforting cobbler. Not to be confused with its British cousin the crumble, cobblers are topped with a scone dumpling rather than a crumbly crust. The addition of cornmeal, which makes for a more toothsome topping, is a clue to the dish's origins in the American South.

SERVES 8

EQUIPMENT: 1 rectangular ovenproof dish, 20 × 30cm

Vanilla ice cream or clotted cream, to serve (optional)

For the plums

750g ripe plums, halved and stoned

50g light brown soft sugar

2 cinnamon sticks

50g stem ginger, finely diced

Juice of 1 lemon

25g unsalted butter, diced

For the cobbler topping

100g plain flour

40g cornmeal

1 teaspoon baking powder

75g unsalted butter, well chilled and cut into 1cm cubes

60ml milk

50ml buttermilk

25g caster sugar

2 tablespoons demerara sugar

1. Toss the plums with the brown sugar in a mixing bowl and set aside to soften for 30 minutes. Meanwhile, preheat the oven to 180°C/160°C fan/Gas Mark 4.

2. Arrange the plums in the ovenproof dish and mix through the cinnamon sticks, ginger and lemon juice. Dot with the butter and bake for 25 minutes until the plums are soft and juicy.

3. While the plums are baking, prepare the cobbler topping. Mix the flour, cornmeal and baking powder together in a mixing bowl or a food processor. Add the butter and rub in with your fingertips or pulse in the food processor until the mixture resembles breadcrumbs. Then mix in the milk, buttermilk and caster sugar to form a dough, by hand using a spoon so that you don't overwork the dough.

4. Remove the plums from the oven and pick out the cinnamon sticks, which have done their job. Roll the dough into golf ball-sized balls, flatten them into 2cm-thick discs between the palms of your hands and then arrange them over the top of the plums, leaving gaps between the dough discs for the plums to peek through. Sprinkle the top with the demerara sugar and bake for 35–40 minutes until puffed up and golden.

5. Remove from the oven and leave to cool for 5 minutes before serving with vanilla ice cream or clotted cream, if liked.

TIP

IF YOU CAN'T FIND BUTTERMILK, USE 75ML NATURAL YOGURT MIXED WITH 25ML MILK FOR A SIMILAR RESULT.

FIG & ALMOND FRANGIPANE

I've always thought 'frangipane' to be a wonderful word – almost as satisfying to say as it is to eat. Here, the traditional sweet, nutty filling is tempered by some rather grown-up figs, slowly stewed in rich red wine. Be careful who you serve this to, as they may start turning up unannounced.

SERVES 8

EQUIPMENT: 1 × 23cm round loose-bottomed fluted tart tin

For the pastry

200g plain flour, plus a little extra for dusting

40g icing sugar

100g unsalted butter, well chilled and cut into 1cm cubes

50g ground almonds

Small pinch of fine sea salt

Grated zest of 1 unwaxed orange

1 egg, beaten

For the frangipane filling

150g unsalted butter, softened

150g light muscovado sugar

3 eggs

150g ground almonds

1 tablespoon plain flour

Grated zest and juice of 1 unwaxed lemon

8 figs, quartered

50g clear honey

For the stewed figs

3 tablespoons light brown soft sugar

100ml red wine

6 figs, quartered

Continued overleaf >>

1. First, make the pastry. Sift the flour and icing sugar together into a mixing bowl or a food processor. Add the butter and rub in with your fingertips or pulse in the food processor until the mixture resembles fine breadcrumbs. Add the ground almonds, salt, orange zest and beaten egg, and mix with a round-bladed knife or pulse until the mixture just comes together to form a dough, adding a couple of tablespoons of ice-cold water if it's too dry. Turn the pastry out onto a lightly floured surface and knead very briefly into a ball. Pat into a wide, 3cm-thick disc, wrap in cling film and leave to rest in the fridge for an hour.

2. Roll the pastry out on a lightly floured surface into a circle about 3mm thick and line your tin with it, making sure the edges of the pastry stand a little proud above the rim of the tin. Trim the edges to even, prick the base all over with a fork and chill the pastry case in the fridge for 30 minutes. Don't be tempted to skip this step, as it helps prevent the pastry shrinking when baked.

3. Meanwhile, preheat the oven to 180°C/160°C fan/Gas Mark 4.

4. Line the pastry case with a piece of non-stick baking paper and fill it with dried beans, uncooked rice or ceramic baking beans. Bake the pastry case on the middle shelf of the oven for 15 minutes. Remove the paper and baking beans or rice and then bake the pastry case for a further 15 minutes to crisp up the base. Remove from the oven and set aside to cool, leaving the oven on.

5. To make the frangipane, beat the butter and sugar together in a stand mixer fitted with the paddle attachment or in a large mixing bowl with an electric whisk until light and fluffy. Add the eggs, one by one, beating after each addition to incorporate. Then fold in the ground almonds, flour and lemon zest and juice.

Continued overleaf >>

For the whipped mascarpone

150g mascarpone cheese

3 tablespoons icing sugar

1 tablespoon vanilla paste

6. Scrape the frangipane into the cooled pastry case, then arrange the fig quarters over the top, pushing them into the frangipane as you go. Bake for 40 minutes until a skewer inserted into the centre of the frangipane comes out clean. Remove from the oven, and while the tart is still warm, brush over the honey. Leave to cool in the tin for 20 minutes before removing.

7. To prepare the stewed figs, heat the sugar in a saucepan over a medium–low heat until it just starts to catch and melt at the sides. Pour in the red wine (it will spit a little) and boil for 2–3 minutes until the mixture thickens slightly and turns glossy. Stir in the figs and let them warm through and soften for a minute before removing the pan from the heat.

8. Whip the mascarpone with the icing sugar and vanilla paste in a mixing bowl with an electric whisk until it's light and airy. Once the tart is completely cool, slice into 8 and serve each slice with a dollop of the mascarpone and a little of the stewed figs on the side.

CROWD-PLEASING CHOCOLATE STACK CAKE

Very few puds with this level of wow factor are so simple to make. Essentially, this is
a cheat's roulade in that, rather than carefully rolling the sponge cake into a spiral
(always a will-it-won't-it moment), it's served as a layer cake. But forget any ideas of nice,
dainty slices – this is a cake to enjoy messily with spoons.

SERVES 8–10
EQUIPMENT: 3 large baking sheets

For the cakes

200g dark chocolate (at least 70% cocoa
solids), broken into squares

6 eggs, separated

200g caster sugar, plus 3 tablespoons
for sprinkling

1 teaspoon vanilla extract or paste

75g plain flour

25g cocoa powder

For the cream filling

250ml double cream

15g icing sugar

1 teaspoon vanilla extract or paste

300g mixed berries (I like blueberries,
blackberries and raspberries)

1. Preheat the oven to 180°C/160°C fan/Gas Mark 4.

2. To make the cakes, place the chocolate in a heatproof bowl set
   over a saucepan of gently simmering water, making sure the
   base of the bowl doesn't touch the water, and stir occasionally
   until it has just melted. Set aside to cool for 5 minutes.

3. Whisk the egg yolks, caster sugar and vanilla extract or paste
   together in a stand mixer fitted with the whisk attachment
   or in a large mixing bowl with an electric whisk until pale
   and thick. Sift over the flour and cocoa powder and beat to
   combine. In a separate mixing bowl, whisk the egg whites with
   a clean electric whisk until soft peaks form.

4. Mix the cooled melted chocolate (it should be no hotter than
   body temperature) into the egg yolk mixture, then fold in a
   spoonful of the whisked egg whites to loosen the mixture.
   Fold the remaining egg whites into the chocolate mixture in
   3 batches, incorporating each addition until no white bits are
   visible before adding the next.

5. Cut 3 sheets of non-stick baking paper to line the 3 large
   baking sheets. Draw an 18cm circle on one sheet of paper
   (you can use a plate of the right size as a guide), then use that
   to trace a circle on each of the other 2 sheets. Sprinkle each
   circle with a tablespoon of caster sugar. Pour one-third of the
   chocolate mixture into the centre of each circle and use a
   spatula to spread it out to fill the circle evenly.

6. Place each baking sheet on a separate oven shelf and bake
   the cakes for 12–15 minutes, checking after 10 minutes and
   swapping the sheets around so that they bake evenly. The cakes
   are done when they are firm to the touch and dry on top.

Continued overleaf >>

7. Remove from the oven and leave the cakes to cool on the sheets for 5 minutes before lifting them, still on the lining paper, and transferring them to a wire rack to cool completely (this helps the sponge to remain fudgy).

8. While the cakes are cooling, make the filling by whipping the cream with the icing sugar and vanilla extract or paste in a mixing bowl with the electric whisk until soft peaks form.

9. To construct the cake stack, peel away the baking paper from one of the chocolate cakes and stand the cake on a serving platter. Spread one-third of the filling over the cake and scatter over a handful of berries. Repeat with the remaining cakes and filling, finishing with a swoop of the cream mixture over the top of the cake. Arrange the rest of the berries over the top (taking care now, as this is the bit that people will see). Serve at the table for everyone to help themselves.

TIP

I FIND IT USEFUL TO GET AHEAD WHEN I AM ENTERTAINING AND THESE CAKES FREEZE WELL. AT THE END OF STEP 5 MAKE SURE THE CAKES HAVE COOLED COMPLETELY, THEN TAKE EACH LAYER, INTERLEAVE WITH SOME NON-STICK BAKING PAPER, PILE INTO A STACK AND WRAP IN CLINGFILM. CAREFULLY PLACE THE STACK OF CAKES INTO A LARGE FREEZER BAG BEFORE FREEZING.

TO USE, REMOVE FROM THE FREEZER A MINIMUM OF 3 HOURS BEFORE YOU NEED THEM, UNWRAP AND ALLOW THE CAKES TO THAW OUT. FOLLOW STEPS 6 AND 7 TO ASSEMBLE THE CAKE.

FRUIT & NUT COOKIE

If the idea of a cookie that serves up to ten people is attractive to you, all I can say is that I salute you, and it's likely that your guests will too. Gargantuan, normally a gross overstatement whatever the context, feels almost timid here. Once cooked, just plonk the pan on the table, top with some good ice cream, give everyone a spoon and enjoy your new status as a total legend.

SERVES 8–10

EQUIPMENT: 1 × 28cm ovenproof non-stick frying pan

200g unsalted butter, softened

200g light brown soft sugar

100g golden caster sugar

1 large egg

1 teaspoon vanilla extract

300g plain flour

25g cocoa powder

1 teaspoon baking powder

½ teaspoon bicarbonate of soda

½ teaspoon sea salt

200g chocolate, a mixture of white and dark, chopped into bite-sized chunks

75g unblanched hazelnuts, very roughly chopped

100g dried figs, very roughly chopped

Ice cream, to serve

1. Preheat the oven to 180°C/160°C fan/Gas Mark 4.

2. Beat the butter and sugars together in a stand mixer fitted with the paddle attachment or in a mixing bowl with an electric whisk until light and fluffy. Then beat in the egg and vanilla extract.

3. Sift the flour, cocoa powder, baking powder and bicarbonate of soda together into a separate mixing bowl, then scrunch the sea salt over. Stir the dry ingredients into the butter, sugar and egg mixture to form a dough.

4. Fold all the flavouring ingredients into the cookie dough until evenly incorporated.

5. Scoop the cookie dough into the ovenproof frying pan and roughly flatten using the back of a spoon. Bake for 20 minutes until slightly puffed.

6. Remove from the oven and leave to cool for 5–10 minutes (being cautious of the hot frying pan handle), then place the cookie, still in the pan, in the centre of the table with ice cream and a handful of spoons for sharing.

GOOSEBERRY FOOL IN 5

This might well take the prize for Easiest Pud Ever – you can have it on the table in minutes and with very little effort. Canned gooseberries are fabulous, but they do vary in zippiness, so feel free to buoy up the syrup with a spoonful or two of sugar, should it be necessary. If you're feeling cheeky, some crushed ginger biscuits make a wonderfully crunchy topping.

SERVES 4

400g can gooseberries in syrup
200ml double cream
100ml Greek yogurt
1–3 tablespoons caster sugar (optional)

1. Pour the gooseberries into a sieve set over a large mixing bowl to catch the syrup. Place the gooseberries in a small mixing bowl and use a fork to crush them gently and burst them open. Set aside.

2. Pour the cream into a large mixing bowl and whip with an electric whisk until stiff peaks form and it holds its shape. Fold in the Greek yogurt and half the reserved syrup, then taste and add sugar if you prefer it a little sweeter.

3. Fold in the crushed gooseberries to create a ripple effect, reserving a few for decorating. Spoon the fool into glasses, then place the reserved gooseberries on top of the cream and use the tip of a spoon to pull them through so that you can see a shock of green among the cream.

4. Cover the fools and chill in the fridge for at least an hour before serving with teaspoons.

CHOCOLATE BEET BROWNIE CUPS

Deep, earthy, slightly sweet beetroot pairs surprisingly well with rich, slightly bitter dark chocolate. And, as always, hiding veg in a pud this delicious is always a thrill. The crucial thing here is to fold the beaten egg whites carefully into the melted chocolate mixture, rather than simply stirring them together, which would knock the air out and undo all of your good work.

MAKES 12 brownie cups
EQUIPMENT: 1 × 12-hole muffin tin

200g cooked, peeled beetroot

200g dark chocolate (at least 70% cocoa solids), broken into squares

100g unsalted butter, diced, plus a little extra for greasing

4 tablespoons cocoa powder (or 2 tablespoons if using paper muffin cases), sifted, plus extra to decorate

3 eggs, separated

100g caster sugar

Grated zest of 1 unwaxed orange

1 teaspoon vanilla extract

Pinch of salt

Cream or ice cream, to serve

1. Preheat the oven to 180°C/160°C fan/Gas Mark 4.

2. Grease the muffin tin with butter and dust with 2 tablespoons of the cocoa powder, or line with paper muffin cases.

3. Grate the beetroot finely on a box grater. Transfer the grated beetroot to a sieve over the sink and leave to drain.

4. Place the chocolate with the butter in a heatproof bowl set over a saucepan of barely simmering water, making sure the base of the bowl doesn't touch the water, and stir occasionally until it is almost all melted; the remainder will melt in the residual heat. Set aside to cool.

5. Whisk the egg whites and sugar together in a stand mixer fitted with the whisk attachment or in a large mixing bowl with an electric whisk until bright white, glossy and forming stiff peaks. This should take you about 5 minutes in the stand mixer, longer with a hand whisk.

6. Beat the egg yolks into the cooled chocolate mixture with the drained beetroot until combined, then add a spoonful of the whisked egg whites to the chocolate bowl and fold in gently (don't beat!) until fully incorporated. Add the remaining whisked egg whites to the chocolate mixture and gently fold in again until no white bits are visible. Finally, fold in the remaining 2 tablespoons of cocoa powder, the orange zest, vanilla extract and salt.

7. Pour the mixture into the muffin holes and stand the muffin tin in a deep roasting tin. Fill a kettle with water and bring to the boil, then pour the boiling water around the muffin tin until it comes halfway up the sides.

8. Bake the muffins for 30 minutes until cracked on top but with a bit of wobble in the middle. Remove from the oven and lift the muffin tin out of the roasting tin, then leave the muffins to cool in the tin for a couple of minutes before lifting them out with a spatula and serving warm with a dollop of cream or ice cream on the side and a sprinkling of cocoa powder to decorate.

SPELT DIGESTIVES

A couple of clever substitutions move these homemade biscuits into a completely different league from the classic, shop-bought digestive (as nice as those are). Spelt is nuttier and slightly sweeter than its modern cousin wheat, and the coconut sugar has a rich, almost toffee-apple flavour. These are fab with an ice-cold aperitivo, sliced figs and some strong blue cheese.

MAKES ABOUT 30 biscuits
EQUIPMENT: 5cm round cookie cutter

80g rolled porridge oats
150g wholegrain spelt flour, plus a little extra for dusting
½ tablespoon baking powder
Pinch of salt
115g unsalted butter, softened
70g coconut sugar
2 tablespoons milk
60g raisins, roughly chopped

1. Add the oats, flour, baking powder and salt to a food processor and blitz for a minute or so until the mixture resembles breadcrumbs. Add the butter and sugar and blitz for a further minute. Finally, add the milk and the raisins to the food processor and pulse until the mixture just begins to come together into a dough.

2. Spoon the mixture out of the food processor and, using floured hands, bring it together to form a dough. Wrap in cling film and chill in the fridge for 30 minutes.

3. Preheat the oven to 180°C/160°C fan/Gas Mark 4. Line 2 baking sheets with non-stick baking paper.

4. Roll the dough out on a floured surface to a large round about 3mm thick. Cut out rounds from the dough using the cutter, re-rolling the trimmings and cutting out more rounds until all the dough is used up.

5. Arrange the dough rounds on the lined baking sheets roughly 2cm apart and bake for 10–12 minutes until they are just beginning to brown. Remove from the oven and leave to cool for 10 minutes on the sheets before transferring to a wire rack to cool completely.

TIP

IF YOU FIND COCONUT SUGAR DIFFICULT TO SOURCE, REPLACE IT WITH GOLDEN CASTER SUGAR.

RASPBERRY, CHOCOLATE & ALMOND DUTCH BABY

Dutch baby is an odd name for a pud, I'll give you that. But it's just an oven-baked pancake, not unlike a big, sweet Yorkshire pudding. And what's not to love about that? Despite the name, it has nothing to do with Holland. The Pennsylvania Dutch are, perhaps confusingly, a German American community. One that knows a thing or two about good desserts, it would seem.

SERVES 6

EQUIPMENT: 1 × 25cm ovenproof non-stick frying pan, or you could use a rectangular roasting tin, 21 × 28cm, 4cm deep

For the chocolate sauce

200g dark chocolate (at least 70% cocoa solids), broken into squares

200ml milk

2 tablespoons double cream

30g caster sugar

30g unsalted butter, chilled and cut into small cubes

For the Dutch baby

125g plain flour

1 tablespoon caster sugar

4 large eggs

250ml milk

½ teaspoon salt

1 teaspoon almond extract

25g unsalted butter, melted

To serve

400g seasonal fruit, such as raspberries, cherries or quartered figs, warmed

100g icing sugar, plus a little extra for dusting

1. First, make the chocolate sauce. Place the chocolate in a heatproof bowl set over a saucepan of gently simmering water, making sure the base of the bowl doesn't touch the water, and stir occasionally until it has just melted.

2. Meanwhile, place the milk, cream and sugar in a saucepan and stir over a low heat until the sugar has dissolved.

3. Once the chocolate has melted, pour it into the warm milk mixture and beat together. Remove the pan from the heat and, using a wooden spoon, beat in the cold butter a cube at a time until the sauce is smooth and glossy. Set aside and keep warm.

4. Preheat the oven to 220°C/200°C fan/Gas Mark 7 with your ovenproof pan inside to heat up while you prepare the batter and seasonal fruit.

5. Add the seasonal fruit to a mixing bowl with the icing sugar. Stir to combine and set aside.

6. To prepare the Dutch baby, add all the ingredients, reserving half the melted butter, to a blender or food processor and blend for about 30 seconds until smooth.

7. Remove the hot pan from the oven, add the reserved melted butter and swirl the pan to coat the base, then carefully pour in the batter. Place the pan on the highest oven shelf and bake the pancake for 18–20 minutes until it is deep golden brown and puffed up around the edges.

8. Remove from the oven and spoon the seasonal fruit into the centre of the pancake, then leave to cool slightly before dusting with icing sugar and serving in slices with the hot chocolate sauce.

TIP

A WORD OF WARNING: RESIST OPENING THE OVEN DOOR WHILE THE DUTCH BABY IS COOKING, OTHERWISE IT WILL BE IN DANGER OF COLLAPSE!

COURGETTE & LEMON POPPY SEED BARS

I don't know about you, but I always get great satisfaction from sneaking veg into sweet treats. It's a sly way of making them a little less naughty, which in itself feels like quite a naughty thing to do. The contrast of the sweet shortbread base and the super-lemony courgette layer is what makes these bars so special.

MAKES 12 bars
EQUIPMENT: 1 × 20cm square baking tin

For the shortbread base

200g unsalted butter, well chilled and cut into 1cm cubes, plus a little extra for greasing

100g caster sugar

200g plain flour

100g cornflour

Grated zest of 1 unwaxed lemon

½ teaspoon fine sea salt

For the courgette cake layer

4 eggs

200g caster sugar

1 large courgette (about 200g), finely grated

Grated zest and juice of 3 unwaxed lemons

100g ground almonds

100g plain flour

40g poppy seeds

For the lemon drizzle

125g icing sugar

2–3 tablespoons freshly squeezed lemon juice

Grated zest of 1 unwaxed lemon

1. Preheat the oven to 200°C/180°C fan/Gas Mark 6. Lightly grease the baking tin with butter.

2. To make the shortbread base, add the butter and sugar to a food processor and pulse together until completely combined and looking like a thick dough. Sift in the flour and cornflour and add the lemon zest along with the sea salt. Pulse again to combine and then check that the mixture comes together when you pinch it between your fingers.

3. Tip the shortbread mixture into the greased tin and use a spatula to press it down into an even layer. Prick all over with a fork and bake for 20–22 minutes until golden.

4. While the shortbread base is baking, make the cake layer. Whisk the eggs and sugar together in a stand mixer fitted with the whisk attachment or in a large mixing bowl with an electric whisk until light and fluffy. Add the remaining ingredients and whisk again.

5. Remove the shortbread from the oven and leave to cool for at least 5 minutes before pouring over the courgette layer.

6. Reduce the oven temperature to 190°C/170°C fan/Gas Mark 5 and bake for 40 minutes until set in the centre and deep golden on top.

7. Remove from the oven and leave to cool completely in the tin before cutting into 12 rectangular-shaped bars.

8. For the lemon drizzle, stir the icing sugar and lemon juice together in a small bowl until well combined. Use a teaspoon to drizzle this over the bars, then top with the grated lemon zest.

CARROT CAKE DROP SCONES

If you have a reasonably well-stocked store cupboard and a carrot lurking in
the fridge, you'll be able to knock up these dainty little drop scones without venturing
to the shops. The carrot gives texture, sweetness and a vague nod to health (items such
as drop scones should only ever nod to health – and always vaguely). Make the batter
up to an hour in advance and fry to order.

MAKES 12 scones

225g plain flour

2 teaspoons baking powder

Pinch of salt

1 teaspoon ground allspice

1 teaspoon ground cinnamon, plus
a little extra for dusting

2 tablespoons light brown soft sugar

30g unsalted butter, melted and slightly
cooled, plus extra for frying

2 large eggs, separated

275ml semi-skimmed milk

1 large carrot, peeled and coarsely grated

45g raisins

To serve

Thick natural yogurt

Clear honey

1. Sift the flour, baking powder, salt and spices into a large mixing bowl. Add the sugar and mix the ingredients together, then make a well in the centre. Add the melted butter, egg yolks and milk to the well and use a wooden spoon to gradually beat the liquid ingredients into the dry ingredients until you have a smooth batter. Stir through the grated carrot and raisins.

2. Whisk the egg whites in a stand mixer fitted with the whisk attachment or in a separate mixing bowl with an electric whisk until stiff peaks form. Fold the egg whites into the batter and gently stir to combine, being careful not to beat the air out of the batter.

3. Heat a non-stick frying pan or flat griddle over a medium heat. Add a knob of butter, and once it has melted, add a large spoonful of the batter mixture. Cook for a couple of minutes, just until tiny bubbles appear on the surface of the scone, then flip over and cook on the other side for 2–3 minutes.

4. Serve immediately with a dollop of natural yogurt, a drizzle of honey and a sprinkling of cinnamon.

TIP

YOU CAN MAKE AND COOK THE DROP SCONES THE DAY BEFORE, COVER
AND STORE IN THE FRIDGE OVERNIGHT AND THEN SIMPLY REHEAT TO ORDER
IN A HOT DRY FRYING PAN.

OVEN-DRIED APPLE CRISPS

Slowly drying out thin slices of apple in a low oven not only results in an addictive crispness but also concentrates the fruit's flavour and natural sweetness, making for an even more appley apple taste. The method below works with other fruit too – mango, for example, or even pineapple. But do adjust your baking time accordingly, as these fruits contain more water than apples tend to, so will need a little longer in the oven. These crisps are a fun way to get one of your five-a-day.

SERVES 4

EQUIPMENT: 3 large baking sheets and 3 oven shelves; mandoline slicer or spiralizer with mandoline attachment

2 firm red-skinned apples, such as Braeburn

Large pinch of ground cinnamon, allspice or ginger (optional)

1. Preheat the oven to 120°C/100°C fan/Gas Mark ½. Line your 3 baking sheets with non-stick baking paper.

2. Core the apples, then use a mandoline or the mandoline attachment on a spiralizer to cut them into 1mm-thick slices.

3. Lay the apple slices out on the lined baking sheets without overlapping, then sprinkle with the spice, if using.

4. Place each baking sheet on a separate oven shelf and bake the apple slices for an hour, opening the oven every 15 minutes to release the steam and turning the apple slices once after 30 minutes.

5. Turn the oven off and leave the apple slices in the oven for an hour until completely cooled. Remove from the oven and transfer the apple slices to a wire rack to crisp up. The crisps should keep well in an airtight container for a week.

ROASTED RHUBARB

Realizing you have a batch of roasted rhubarb squirrelled away at the back of the fridge is a most comforting thought. Not only is it super-handy for impromptu puds with the addition of custard, whipped cream or ice cream, it will take your breakfasts up a notch too, served with a dollop or two of thick Greek yogurt and a generous sprinkling of crunchy granola.

SERVES 6–8

1kg rhubarb, forced if available (see tip)
100g caster sugar
Juice of ½ lemon

Flavour boosters (optional)

• Rind of ½ unwaxed orange, pared in strips
• Rind of ½ unwaxed lemon, pared in strips
• 1cm piece of stem ginger, finely chopped
• 1 vanilla pod, split lengthways
• 2 teaspoons orange blossom water
• A few sprigs of thyme
• 2 tablespoons clear honey (use 30g less sugar)
• 6 cardamom pods
• 1 cinnamon stick

1. Preheat the oven to 200°C/180°C fan/Gas Mark 6.

2. Rinse the rhubarb stalks and shake off any excess water, then cut them into 3cm pieces. Toss in a large shallow roasting tin with the sugar and lemon juice to coat each piece evenly with sugar. Mix through any optional flavour boosters before covering the tin tightly with foil. Roast on the middle shelf of the oven for 15 minutes.

3. Remove from the oven and lift away the foil. By now the sugar should have melted. Roast the rhubarb, uncovered, for a final 15 minutes until it's completely soft but still holds its shape.

4. Remove from the oven and leave to cool. Transfer the rhubarb with all its syrup to a bowl or other container, cover and store in the fridge for up to a week.

TIP

FORCED RHUBARB IS USUALLY AVAILABLE FROM WINTER TO EARLY SPRING, ALTHOUGH SOME SUPERMARKETS HAVE STARTED TO STOCK IT THROUGHOUT THE YEAR. DO TRY AND GET HOLD OF IT IF YOU CAN; ITS BRILLIANT JEWEL-LIKE PINK COLOUR LOOKS ALMOST UNNATURAL, BUT IT'S A PURE PLEASURE TO COOK WITH.

PASTRY, DRESSINGS & USEFUL STUFF

SAVOURY SHORTCRUST PASTRY

Traditional shortcrust pastry is made up of two parts plain flour to one part fat, such as butter, plus a tiny amount of cold water. At Higgidy, we've had lots of practice making shortcrust pastry, so here is our trusted recipe, which is both delicious and easy to handle. For the ultimate savoury flavour, we add cheese. This makes the pastry taste great and gives it a gorgeous golden colour when baked, but you can leave it out if you prefer a more traditional approach. To make a richer pastry, add a touch more butter and an egg yolk. The pastry can be made easily by hand or using a food processor.

MAKES 350g

200g plain flour, plus a little extra for dusting
Generous pinch of salt
100g butter, well chilled and cut into 1cm cubes
30g Parmesan cheese, grated (optional)
1 egg yolk, beaten
About 3 tablespoons ice-cold water

How it's done – by hand

1. Sift the flour and salt into a large mixing bowl.

2. Add the butter and lightly rub in with your fingertips until the mixture resembles breadcrumbs.

3. Add the Parmesan, if using, and rub again until the cheese is mixed in evenly.

4. Add the beaten egg yolk and measured ice-cold water and mix with a round-bladed knife until the mixture just comes together to form a dough.

5. Turn the pastry out onto a lightly floured surface and knead very briefly into a ball. Try not to handle it too much at this stage, or the butter will get warm and the pastry will become tricky to use and may turn out tough and chewy.

6. Wrap in cling film and leave to rest in the fridge for 30 minutes before using.

How it's done – in a food processor

Making shortcrust pastry in a food processor takes just minutes. Pulse the flour, salt, butter and cheese, if using, together until the mixture resembles breadcrumbs. Add the egg yolk beaten with the ice-cold water and pulse until the mixture just comes together to form a dough, adding a tiny bit more water if you think it's needed. Wrap in cling film and leave to rest in the fridge for 30 minutes.

If you're feeling adventurous...

Once you've mastered the basics of shortcrust pastry you can experiment with adding extra flavours such as nuts, herbs or seeds – see the suggestions below. Stir in once the mixture resembles fine breadcrumbs, just before you add the egg yolk and water. Be aware that some additions, such as moist herbs or oily nuts, can make the pastry harder to handle. Try the following:

- A tablespoon of finely chopped fresh herbs – woody herbs such as thyme, rosemary and oregano work best. Avoid wetter herbs like chives or parsley, and remember to remove any stalks before chopping.

- A couple of teaspoons of seeds, such as sesame, poppy, black onion (nigella) or caraway. These add flavour and texture to the pastry. The darker-coloured seeds look really pretty too.

- Spices, such as a pinch of saffron threads, paprika or dried chilli flakes. These taste delicious and give the pastry a beautiful colour.

- 40–50g finely chopped walnuts, pecan nuts or hazelnuts. You can add these to both savoury and sweet shortcrust pastry.

- Grated unwaxed lemon, lime or orange zest, to give sweet shortcrust pastry some zing. Use your finest grater to achieve the best distribution through the pastry, and add the zest to the flour before rubbing in the butter.

WALNUTTY PASTRY

Walnuts have always been regarded as brain food not just because they are high in
omega-3 fatty acids, which support brain function, but also because the shell is shaped like
the human skull and the kernel inside resembles the brain. They have a pleasingly earthy taste
and slightly drier texture than some other nuts, which makes them perfect for using in pastry
to add flavour and texture interest. Be careful when blitzing them in a food processor
not go too far and create a sticky butter.

MAKES 400g

40g walnuts

200g plain flour, plus a little extra
for dusting

30g Parmesan cheese, grated

½ teaspoon salt

100g unsalted butter, well chilled
and cut into 1cm cubes

1 egg, beaten

1–2 tablespoons ice-cold water

1. Blitz the walnuts with 2 tablespoons of the flour in a food
processor until finely ground. Add the remaining flour, the
Parmesan and salt and briefly pulse to combine. Then add the
butter and pulse again until the mixture resembles breadcrumbs.
Finally, add the egg beaten with about 1 tablespoon ice-cold
water and pulse until the mixture just comes together to form
a dough, adding the remaining water if needed.

2. Turn the pastry out onto a lightly floured surface and knead
very briefly into a ball, but don't worry if it's a little crumbly.
Pat into a disc, wrap in cling film and leave to rest in the fridge
for 30 minutes before using.

PARMESAN TWISTS

These curly pastry delights are perfect for picnicking or after-school snacking. They're a great way of using up pastry trimmings, as you don't need these to puff up in any uniform fashion. Adding the tomato paste gives the twists a delicious tanginess and a splash of colour too.

MAKES 10 twists

320g ready-rolled all-butter puff pastry, defrosted if frozen, or left-over pastry trimmings

A little plain flour, for dusting

2–3 heaped tablespoons sun-dried tomato paste

60g hard cheese, such as Parmesan or Cheddar, finely grated

1 beaten egg, to glaze

1. Preheat the oven to 220°C/200°C fan/Gas Mark 7. Line a baking sheet with non-stick baking paper.

2. Unroll the pastry on a lightly floured surface. Spread the tomato paste evenly over the pastry sheet and sprinkle the cheese evenly on top.

3. Starting from one long side, fold the pastry sheet in half and then roll it out to about the same size as before (don't worry if some of the paste oozes out). Cut across into 10 strips. Carefully twist each strip 3 or 4 times until it looks like a curly straw.

4. Place the twists on the lined baking sheet and chill in the fridge for 20 minutes.

5. Brush with the beaten egg to glaze and bake for 8–10 minutes or until the pastry is golden brown. These are delicious warm, but can be served at room temperature.

TOMATO HARISSA SAUCE

This vibrant, slightly smoky-flavoured sauce can be used as a dip or smothered over some cooked veggies, or even served alongside grilled halloumi cheese and other mezze bits and pieces.

MAKES 200ml

2 tomatoes

1 large garlic clove, crushed

Grated zest and juice of ½ unwaxed lemon, plus more juice to taste if needed

½ green chilli, deseeded and finely chopped

1 teaspoon harissa paste

3 tablespoons olive oil

Pinch of salt, plus more to taste

1. Finely chop the tomatoes, seeds and all, and decant into a bowl with their juices.

2. Add the remaining ingredients, seasoning with the pinch of salt, and stir to combine. Taste the sauce and season with more salt, plus a touch more lemon juice if needed.

TIP

IF YOU'RE FINDING HARISSA TRICKY TO FIND, SWITCH IT FOR A TEASPOON OF SMOKED PAPRIKA AND A PINCH OF CHILLI POWDER.

TAHINI SAUCE

I know the word 'drizzle' is unfashionable but that's what this sauce is so good for. I serve it with Lebanese-inspired meals such as the Charred Little Gems with Mixed Grains, Falafel & Tahini Sauce on page 47 or with flatbreads (see the recipe on page 163 to make your own).

MAKES 200–250ml, depending on thickness

4 tablespoons light tahini

2 teaspoons light soy sauce

Juice of 1 lemon

½ teaspoon clear honey

Freshly ground black pepper

1. Place all the ingredients except the pepper in a small mixing bowl and whisk together to combine. The mixture will seize and thicken as the lemon juice reacts with the tahini, so whisk in up to 5 tablespoons of water, a tablespoon at a time, until the mixture resembles very thick double cream. Season to taste with pepper.

2. This will keep in a sterilized glass jar in the fridge for a couple of weeks, during which time it might stiffen up, but it can quickly be resurrected with a couple of tablespoons of hot water and a vigorous stir.

BRIGHT GREEN HERB OIL

Herb oils are super-versatile and can miraculously bring a plate of struggling vegetables to life. This one is a wonderful bright green colour, but it will dull after 2–3 hours, so it's not one to make a day ahead. I use it as a dressing for salads or stirred through some simply cooked fresh pasta.

MAKES 200ml

Grated zest and juice of 1 unwaxed lemon
2 garlic cloves, sliced
1 small bunch of coriander, leaves picked
1 small bunch of mint, leaves picked
1 tablespoon white vinegar
100ml olive oil
Salt and freshly ground black pepper

1. Simply blitz all the ingredients in a blender to a thick, green oil.

2. Season the herb oil to taste with salt and pepper before decanting into a bowl.

MINT RAITA

I had to include a recipe for a raita, as a dollop of cooling lightly spiced minty yogurt is my go-to accompaniment for any Indian- or North African-inspired meal. This would be great with the Stuffed Bulgur Aubergine with Chermoula on page 74.

MAKES 300ml

½ teaspoon cumin seeds
½ teaspoon black peppercorns
250g natural yogurt
1 large garlic clove, crushed
40g mint, leaves picked
10g coriander, leaves picked
Pinch of salt

1. Using a pestle and mortar, grind the cumin seeds and black peppercorns to a fine powder.

2. Tip the ground spices into a blender with 2 tablespoons of the yogurt and all the remaining ingredients and blend to a smooth paste. Transfer the paste to a bowl and stir through the remaining yogurt.

TIP

YOU WILL NEED A LARGE BUNCH OF MINT TO GET THE BEST RESULT.

SALSA VERDE

This salsa is featured in the Maple-glazed Parsnip, Cavolo Nero & Pomegranate Salad on page 111 as well as the Ancient Grain Salad on page 46, but it's also brilliant for drizzling over rice, toasted couscous and roasted vegetable dishes. It's a more piquant alternative to pesto and ideal for livening up suppers and lunchboxes. Make a double batch and store in a sterilized glass jar in the fridge for up to a week.

MAKES 150ml

3 cornichons or 10 pitted green olives, drained

2 tablespoons capers in brine, drained

3 tablespoons olive oil

1 garlic clove, peeled

1 small bunch of mixed soft herbs (I use mint, basil and flat leaf parsley), leaves picked

Grated zest and juice of 1 unwaxed lemon

Salt and freshly ground black pepper

1. Blitz all the ingredients in a food processor until you have a chunky paste.

2. Taste and adjust the seasoning, adding more lemon juice or salt depending on your preference. Set aside until you're ready to use or serve.

GREMOLATA

Gremolata is an Italian invention typically including fresh lemon zest, raw garlic, parsley and anchovy. It is the traditional accompaniment to the Italian meat dish ossobuco, but I love this sprinkled over a simply cooked bowl of rice or stirred through cooked tagliatelle.

MAKES 300ml

1 small bunch of flat leaf parsley, leaves picked

1–2 garlic cloves, crushed

Grated zest of 1 unwaxed lemon and 3 tablespoons juice

Pinch of dried chilli flakes (optional)

100ml olive oil

Salt and freshly ground black pepper

1. Roughly chop the parsley leaves and tip into a bowl. Add the crushed garlic and lemon zest and juice, and give it all a good stir. Season to taste with salt and pepper and the chilli flakes, if using. Finally, stir in the olive oil.

2. Store in a sterilized glass jar in the fridge for up to a week.

ONION GRAVY

This recipe was created specifically to go with the Cranberry & Porchini Nut Roast on page 89, but I have found myself serving it alongside other recipes too. It's usefully vegan, as sometimes a vegan meal needs a tasty lubricating accompaniment. I tend to make a double batch and freeze half to use with veggie sausages and mash or with a Sunday roast instead of the meat drippings.

SERVES 6-8

2 tablespoons olive oil

6 shallots (about 250g unpeeled weight), finely sliced

A few sprigs of thyme, leaves picked

1 tablespoon plain flour

100ml dry white wine

1 teaspoon Dijon mustard

1½ teaspoons light brown soft sugar

300ml vegetable stock

Salt and freshly ground black pepper

1. Heat the olive oil in a frying pan over a medium heat, add the shallots and thyme with a pinch of salt and sauté for 5 minutes until softened.

2. Reduce the heat to low and cook the shallots for a further 20–30 minutes until they are golden and caramelized.

3. Turn the heat up to medium, stir in the flour and cook, stirring regularly, for 2 minutes. Pour over the wine and cook until the shallots have absorbed most of the liquid. Add the mustard and sugar and stir to combine before pouring in the vegetable stock. Gently simmer for 5 minutes until the sauce has thickened to a gravy consistency. Season to taste with salt and pepper.

STORE-CUPBOARD STAPLES

Keep the following must-have ingredients in store to help transform your veggie recipes.

BREADCRUMBS

Breadcrumbs add body and crunch to dishes. Use Japanese panko for crispy crumbs or any variety for adding structure to veggie pie fillings.

CAPERS AND OLIVES

The salty tang of capers and olives adds a certain bounce and sophistication to dishes that would otherwise require a lengthy list of ingredients or/and cooking time to achieve.

DRIED MUSHROOMS

Mixed dried wild mushrooms and dried porcini mushrooms add a deeply savoury character to vegetarian dishes that would be provided by meat in non-vegetarian recipes. Rehydrate in warm water before using, and save the soaking water to use as a rich stock in sauces and soups.

JARRED BEANS

Gently cooked in smaller batches and carefully seasoned, jarred beans are worth the extra expense. They make a creamy alternative to root vegetable mash and act as a rich foil to vinegary dressings in grain salads.

NUTS

Nuts add richness, texture and flavour to both sweet and savoury dishes, as well as pastry. Choose raw, unsalted nuts and then roast them gently until golden for maximum flavour.

TAHINI

This sesame seed paste makes a fantastic (and incidentally vegan) creamy dressing, but is also a revelation swirled into brownies or drizzled on top of roasted veg. Tahini is a rich source of protein (better, in fact, than most nuts), and is a good source of healthy (unsaturated) fats.

METRIC/IMPERIAL CONVERSION CHARTS

A note on egg size: For UK readers, eggs should be medium unless otherwise specified, which is the equivalent of a large egg in the US.

WEIGHT CONVERSIONS

5g	⅛oz	85g	3oz	250g	9oz	500g	1lb 2oz
10g	¼oz	90g	3¼oz	275g	9¾oz	550g	1lb 4oz
15g	½oz	100g	3½oz	280g	10oz	600g	1lb 5oz
25/30g	1oz	115g	4oz	300g	10½oz	650g	1lb 7oz
35g	1¼oz	125g	4½oz	325g	11½oz	700g	1lb 9oz
40g	1½oz	140g	5oz	350g	12oz	750g	1lb 10oz
50g	1¾oz	150g	5½oz	375g	13oz	800g	1lb 12oz
55g	2oz	175g	6oz	400g	14oz		
60g	2¼oz	200g	7oz	425g	15oz		
70g	2½oz	225g	8oz	450g	1lb		

LIQUID CONVERSIONS

1.25ml	¼ tsp	90ml	6 tbsp	400ml	14fl oz
2.5ml	½ tsp	100ml	3½fl oz	425ml	15fl oz/¾ pint
5ml	1 tsp	125ml	4fl oz	450ml	16fl oz
10ml	2 tsp	150ml	5fl oz/¼ pint	500ml	18fl oz
15ml	1 tbsp/3 tsp/½fl oz	175ml	6fl oz	568ml	1 pint
30ml	2 tbsp/1fl oz	200ml	7fl oz/⅓ pint	600ml	20fl oz
45ml	3 tbsp	225ml	8fl oz	700ml	1¼ pint
50ml	2fl oz	250ml	9fl oz	850ml	1½ pint
60ml	4 tbsp	300ml	10fl oz/½ pint	1 litre	1¾ pint
75ml	5 tbsp/2½fl oz	350ml	12fl oz		

OVEN TEMPERATURES

150ºC	300ºF
160ºC	325ºF
180ºC	350ºF
190ºC	375ºF
200ºC	400ºF
220ºC	425ºF
230ºC	450ºF

GLOSSARY OF UK & US TERMS

aubergine	eggplant
(non-stick) baking paper	parchment paper
baking sheet	cookie sheet
baking tray	baking sheet
beef tomato	beefsteak tomato
beetroot	beet
bicarbonate of soda	baking soda
biscuit	cookie
broad beans	fava beans
butter beans	lima beans
celeriac	celery root
(Swiss) chard	silverbeet
chickpeas	garbanzo beans
cling film	plastic wrap
coriander, fresh	cilantro
cornflour	cornstarch
courgettes	zucchini
dark chocolate	bittersweet chocolate
double cream	heavy cream
electric whisk	electric mixer
filo pastry	phyllo pastry
flour: plain, strong, wholemeal	all-purpose, bread, whole wheat
frying pan	skillet
ginger biscuits	gingersnaps
greaseproof paper	wax paper
griddle pan	grill pan
grill/grilling	broiler/broiling
hob	stove
kitchen paper	paper towels
mangetout	snow peas
(muffin) paper cases	paper liners
light muscovado sugar	light brown sugar
natural yogurt	plain yogurt
pepper	bell pepper
rocket	arugula
salad leaves	salad greens
(oven) shelf	(oven) rack
shortcrust pastry	pie crust dough
skewer	toothpick
spring onion	scallion/green onion
starter	appetizer
stick blender	immersion blender
stone	pit
swede	rutabaga
Tenderstem broccoli	broccolini
toffee apple	candy apple
tin	pan
tomato purée	tomato paste

INDEX

ACKNOWLEDGEMENTS

'HOW DO YOU MAKE A GOOD MOLEHILL?' ASKED THE BOY.

'BY MAKING A LOT OF BAD ONES FIRST,' SAID THE MOLE.

CHARLIE MACKESY

At Higgidy we create, test, eat and repeat until we've made something we think tastes good. This is the journey we've been on while creating this book and we wouldn't want it any other way.

Higgidy: The Veggie Cookbook is a collaboration created by a talented group of people who've been prepared to come on the 'create, test, eat and repeat journey' and there have been days when we've all eaten far more than our five-a-day!

Central to the inspiration of this book is the wonderfully patient and generous Anna Shepherd. Thank you for dreaming, cooking and driving literally miles... it was a long, hot summer of cooking.

My sister-in-law, the brilliant Georgina Fuggle. Thank you for always picking up the phone when I've needed you and for writing, testing and juggling your family life to make this book happen. Your creativity is inspiring.

The Greeks – Ariel and Nic. From your veranda in Greece you gently pushed the Higgidy brand along. I love your enthusiasm and humour – you always bring joy to my day!

Lee – you are a legend with words. Thank you for bringing to life all that was in my head.

To the team at Higgidy, who've cheered me on and encouraged this book into existence. Amy, thank you for patiently helping me to organise myself and get the recipes together in some kind of coherent state. Nikki, thank you for testing the trickier ones out on your family, the Cranberry & Porcini Nut Roast wouldn't be nearly as good without your children being 'master tasters'.

Denise and the wonderful team at Octopus, thank you for your patience when I've wobbled and for bringing this book together with love, care and a creative desire that honours Higgidy.

Dan and Tonia, it was a pleasure. Thank you for making shoot days my highlight and for never being offended.

Lastly, my long-suffering family. James, Miss Kate and Jack Jack – I am so grateful to you – together we will eat more veg.